FIVERR FREELANCE MASTERY

BY ABDUL RAUF

"Master Fiverr, Master Your Future. Your Guide to Thrive in Freelance Success.

TABLE OF CONTENTS

Introduction

ABOUT THE AUTHOR

Abdul Rauf

Abdul Rauf is an accomplished freelancer on the Fiverr platform, with extensive experience and expertise in translation and content creation. He began his journey on Fiverr as a keen learner, demonstrating a steadfast commitment to mastering the intricacies of the platform through perseverance and dedication. Over time, he has cultivated a deep understanding of the platform and has become a leading expert in his field.

Abdul Rauf's success story inspires those who aspire to excel in the realm of freelancing. His experience underscores the importance of hard work, dedication, and a passion for one's craft. It is clear that the relentless pursuit of excellence has marked Abdul Rauf's journey on Fiverr, and his example serves as a testament to the power of perseverance and a commitment to continuous improvement. As a multilingual professional, Abdul's proficiency extends across various languages, enabling him to provide top-notch translation services that are sought after by a global clientele. His skill in crafting compelling content, engaging narratives, and attention-grabbing copy has solidified his reputation as a skilled content creator in the digital sphere. In this comprehensive eBook, Abdul Rauf shares his wealth of experience, invaluable tips, and practical guidance, to equip readers with the tools and knowledge needed to excel in the competitive world of Fiverr freelancing.

INTRODUCTION

The freelance industry has witnessed a significant shift towards more flexible and autonomous career options, providing individuals with an opportunity to showcase their unique talents, skills, and expertise to a global audience. Amongst the many platforms designed to cater to freelancers, Fiverr has emerged as a leader, transforming how freelancers connect with clients and offer their services. Fiverr's innovative platform and tools have revolutionized the traditional freelance model, making it easier for freelancers to market themselves, increase their visibility, and access a broader range of clients worldwide

The text describes a comprehensive guide that serves as a roadmap for navigating the intricacies of Fiverr's freelancing ecosystem. The guide is designed to help beginners take their first steps into the world of freelancing and assist seasoned professionals in refining their strategies. The eBook is intended to be a compass through Fiverr's labyrinth, a bustling marketplace where talent meets opportunity.

Fiverr is a platform that offers a wide range of categories, including writing and translation, design, and digital marketing, providing a great opportunity for freelancers to excel. It allows people from all over the world to collaborate, share services, and add value to their work, regardless of their location. In the following pages, we will embark on an enlightening journey together. We'll explore the basics of creating a Fiverr profile, developing engaging gigs, building a reliable reputation, and expanding your freelance business. Whether you're an aspiring translator, a proficient content writer, a creative designer, or a skilled professional in any other field, Fiverr provides opportunities to turn your passion into profit.

Let's explore the strategies, nuances, and secrets to thrive as a Fiverr freelancer. Together, we'll discover endless opportunities where your talent can flourish.

WHAT IS FIVERR?

FIVERR, AN ONLINE MARKETPLACE FOR FREELANCERS, WAS ESTABLISHED IN 2010 WITH A DISTINCTIVE APPROACH THAT ENABLED THEM TO OFFER THEIR SERVICES STARTING AT JUST $5, WHICH IS WHERE THE PLATFORM GOT ITS NAME.

As a result, it quickly gained popularity amongst small business owners and entrepreneurs seeking affordable and convenient solutions for their digital needs. As the platform grew, Fiverr evolved to allow freelancers to offer services at varying price points and complexity levels, including graphic design, writing, programming, marketing, and more. This expansion broadened the platform's appeal to a wider range of clients, from individuals to large corporations. Today, Fiverr is a leading digital marketplace that connects businesses with talented freelancers from around the world. With its user-friendly platform and flexible pricing options, it has become a go-to resource for anyone looking to outsource their digital needs.

Fiverr is a leading online marketplace that offers a user-friendly platform for freelancers to showcase their skills, promote their services, and connect with clients worldwide. The platform's interface is designed to be intuitive and easy to navigate, making it easy for freelancers to create profiles that showcase their expertise and attract potential clients. Clients, in turn, can browse through a wide range of services that are offered by freelancers across different categories and industries.

One of the key advantages of Fiverr is that it provides a range of tools and features that facilitate smooth interactions between freelancers and clients. These tools include communication channels, project management features, and payment processing tools, all of which help to streamline the process of working together. Additionally, Fiverr incorporates a robust rating and review system that allows clients to leave feedback on their experiences with freelancers. This system helps to establish trust and credibility within the Fiverr community, enabling freelancers to build their businesses and attract repeat clients.

Overall, Fiverr is a valuable platform that offers numerous benefits to both freelancers and clients. Freelancers can monetize their skills, expand their client base, and build their businesses, while clients can access a wide range of high-quality services, connect with experienced professionals, and receive excellent customer service. The platform's user-friendly interface, tools, and features make it a convenient and efficient way to bring freelancers and clients together from around the world.

conclusion

The emergence of Fiverr has ushered in a new era for freelancers, as it has opened up a world of opportunities that transcend geographical barriers. The platform has revolutionized how freelancers conduct business, allowing them to leverage their unique skill sets and convert them into profitable ventures. Fiverr's innovative and user-friendly platform, combined with its vast range of services and global outreach, has transformed how freelancers work and interact with clients. The gig economy has seen a meteoric rise in recent years, and Fiverr has played a pivotal role in empowering freelancers to take advantage of the limitless potential of remote work. As a result, Fiverr has become a dynamic force that has enabled freelancers to take charge of their professional destinies and realize their full potential as independent entrepreneurs.

WHY DO PEOPLE USE FIVERR?

Fiverr is a widely popular and trustworthy platform that offers professional services across various domains such as graphic design, copywriting, programming, digital marketing, and more. It stands out from its competitors due to its unparalleled ease of access to a large pool of skilled freelancers who can provide customized solutions to specific needs. Fiverr's convenience is unparalleled as clients can easily find the expertise they require within a few clicks without enduring lengthy hiring processes or commitments. Fiverr's versatility caters to various budgets, enabling both large corporations and small startups to access services at different price points. Fiverr's user-friendly interface simplifies browsing through a multitude of offerings, allowing clients to quickly identify suitable freelancers based on their skills, expertise, and past work. This accessibility fosters trust and reliability among users, making Fiverr the preferred choice for outsourcing requirements. Fiverr's review and rating system adds another layer of quality assurance. Clients can gauge freelancers' proficiency through reviews from previous engagements, instilling confidence in their choices. Additionally, Fiverr's global reach facilitates connections between talents and clients worldwide, transcending geographical barriers and enabling seamless collaboration across borders. In essence, Fiverr's allure lies in its ability to streamline the outsourcing process, providing an efficient platform where individuals and businesses can access specialized skills, foster collaborations, and fulfill their diverse needs with ease and reliability. With its vast pool of talented freelancers, budget-friendly options, and user-friendly interface, Fiverr is undoubtedly one of the best platforms for outsourcing requirements across different domains.

HOW MUCH CAN YOU EARN?

When it comes to earning money on Fiverr, several factors come into play. These include your level of expertise, the niche you specialize in, the quality of your service, the demand for your offerings, and your pricing strategy. Freelancers on Fiverr have the flexibility to set their rates based on the value they provide, allowing for a broad spectrum of potential earnings. Some freelancers earn a supplementary income, while others generate substantial revenues, even reaching full-time income levels. However, it's essential to understand that several factors can influence your earnings on the platform. For instance, your ability to attract clients, deliver high-quality work consistently, and position yourself strategically within your chosen niche are all crucial determinants. Freelancers offering in-demand services or possessing unique skills tend to command higher rates and, consequently, have the potential to earn more. It's important to recognize that success and earnings on Fiverr may take time to build, especially when starting. It often requires dedication, consistent delivery of excellent services, gathering positive reviews, and gradually expanding a client base to increase earning potential. As a freelancer, you need to continuously hone your skills, keep up with industry trends, and offer exceptional services to stay ahead of the competition.

The platform offers freelancers an opportunity to scale their earnings based on their efforts, dedication, and ability to meet client demands effectively. If you're just starting, it's advisable to offer your services at a lower rate to attract clients and build your reputation. As you gain more experience and positive reviews, you can gradually increase your rates and earn more. The key to success on Fiverr is to consistently deliver quality work, communicate effectively with clients, and continuously improve your skills.

OVERVIEW OF FREELANCING ON FIVERR

FREELANCING ON FIVERR IS AN AMAZING OPPORTUNITY FOR PEOPLE WHO WANT TO USE THEIR SKILLS AND EXPERTISE IN THE DIGITAL MARKETPLACE.

Fiverr is a cool platform that lets you offer your talents and services to people all over the world. You can show off your skills and offer a wide range of freelance services. It's a great way to make some extra cash doing what you love. This innovative platform serves as a central hub for freelancers across various fields such as graphic design, writing, programming, and marketing to create profiles, showcase their abilities, and market their services, referred to as "gigs." Clients, in turn, can explore a diverse range of offerings, review freelancers' portfolios, and engage those whose expertise aligns with their requirements. The versatility and accessibility of freelancing on Fiverr are noteworthy. Freelancers have the autonomy to define their services, set pricing structures, and communicate directly with clients, fostering a collaborative and transparent working environment.

Furthermore, Fiverr's user-friendly interface, along with robust tools for communication, order management, and secure payments, streamlines the process for both freelancers and clients. This enables efficient project execution, clear expectations, and a seamless experience for all stakeholders.

In essence, freelancing on Fiverr embodies a modern, agile, and inclusive approach to remote work, providing a fertile ground for freelancers worldwide to showcase their talents, build their brands, and forge mutually beneficial professional relationships in a global marketplace.

WHY FIVERR FOR BEGINNERS?

FIVERR IS A GREAT PLACE FOR BEGINNERS WHO WANT TO START FREELANCING. THERE ARE MANY REASONS FOR THIS. ONE OF THE MAIN BENEFITS IS THAT FIVERR CONNECTS FREELANCERS WITH CLIENTS FROM ALL OVER THE WORLD, WHICH CAN HELP THEM GROW THEIR NETWORK. FIVERR IS ALSO EASY TO USE, HAS A SIMPLE PAYMENT SYSTEM, AND OFFERS SUPPORT SERVICES FOR FREELANCERS. THIS MAKES IT EASIER FOR FREELANCERS TO MANAGE THEIR WORK AND EARN MONEY CONSISTENTLY. OVERALL, FIVERR IS AN ACCESSIBLE, RELIABLE, AND INNOVATIVE PLATFORM THAT IS PERFECT FOR THOSE WHO ARE NEW TO FREELANCING.

1. Accessible Platform for Novices:

Fiverr is an easy-to-use platform that's perfect for new freelancers. The interface is intuitive and straightforward, making it easy to create a profile and craft gig listings without any technical hurdles. Whether you're just starting your freelance journey or you're an experienced freelancer, Fiverr has everything you need to succeed.

2. Opportunities Across Varied Categories:

Fiverr is a platform that offers a wide range of categories for beginners to explore and select their niche expertise. These categories include writing, graphic design, programming, digital marketing, and more. The platform caters to different audiences with different needs. Therefore, the information provided in the text is written in plain and simple language to make it easy to understand.

The text is organized logically, with the most important information mentioned first. Sentences are kept short and only include necessary information to avoid confusion. The text is direct, concise, and flows smoothly to make it easier to read. The language used is simple and familiar, avoiding the use of acronyms, jargon, or legal language. The active voice is preferred to increase clarity, making it easier to understand who is doing what.

3. Global Exposure and Reach: Fiverr has a great feature: its audience is global. This means that freelancers can show their skills to many different types of people from all over the world. This is useful because it means that freelancers don't have to worry about where they live when finding work, and they can find more job opportunities.

4. Flexible Entry Levels and Pricing: Fiverr offers a unique opportunity for entry-level professionals to establish their credentials and set their own entry points. The platform's versatile pricing structure and skill-level determination allows for a low-barrier of entry, enabling beginners to compete and succeed in their respective fields at their own pace.

5. Portfolio Development and Showcasing Talents: For beginners, completing gigs can be a great way to start building their portfolios. Each project they complete serves as a stepping stone towards establishing their credibility and attracting future clients. As they build a strong portfolio showcasing their capabilities, they can increase their chances of landing more gigs and growing their career in their chosen field.

6. Learning Hub for New Freelancers: Fiverr is a great platform for beginners to learn about freelancing. It provides an opportunity to gain firsthand experience and learn critical skills such as time management, client interaction, and delivering high-quality services. As a beginner, you can develop these skills and grow your freelancing career on this platform.

7. Supportive Community and Resources: Fiverr is a platform that understands the importance of community in the world of freelancing. That's why it provides a range of resources to help its users connect, share knowledge, and support each other. Through forums, blog posts, and knowledge-sharing platforms, Fiverr cultivates a supportive and collaborative community that fosters growth and success. In particular, beginners stand to gain a great deal from this community. They can learn from the experiences of seasoned freelancers, who offer guidance and share their challenges and triumphs. From managing client relationships to pricing their services, beginners can access a wealth of knowledge that can help them overcome the hurdles of starting a freelance career.

In addition to this guidance and support, Fiverr also provides a range of resources to help freelancers grow their skills and expand their offerings. From online courses to tools and templates, users can access a range of materials designed to help them succeed.

Overall, Fiverr's approach to community-building is one of its key strengths. By creating a platform that collaboration and knowledge-sharing, it has helped countless freelancers achieve their goals and build successful careers.

8. Constructive Feedback Loop: The platform has a robust feedback and review system that works as a great learning tool for beginners. This system enables newcomers to consistently improve their services by providing them with valuable insights and suggestions. The system works by allowing clients to share their thoughts and experiences on the completed gigs, which helps beginners identify the areas they need to refine in their services and enhance customer satisfaction. The feedback and review system is a great way for beginners to learn from their mistakes, understand customer expectations, and grow their skills to offer better services.

9. Utilization of Platform Tools: Fiverr provides novice users with essential tools, including analytics, promotional features, and communication channels. These resources facilitate the efficient management of gigs and enable users to optimize their profiles for enhanced visibility. Through the utilization of these tools, individuals can improve their performance and achieve their desired business objectives.

10. Monetization of Skills and Growth Opportunities: A platform like Fiverr offers a gateway for beginners to monetize their skills, providing an entry point to turn their talents into sources of income while creating opportunities for growth, skill enhancement, and long-term success in the freelancing industry.

In essence: Fiverr is a comprehensive platform that provides a gateway for beginners to dive into the freelancing world. It offers a wide range of opportunities for individuals to explore their skills and find suitable projects in their areas of interest. The platform provides an ecosystem that is conducive to learning, growth, and development of skills. It provides a safe and secure environment for freelancers to showcase their talents and connect with clients from all over the world. Fiverr also offers various resources, tools, and support to help freelancers succeed in their chosen fields. From personalized dashboards to tailored recommendations, Fiverr has everything that a freelancer needs to realize the full potential of their skills. Overall, Fiverr is an excellent platform for anyone looking to start their freelancing career or take it to the next level.

GETTING STARTED ON FIVERR

"GETTING STARTED ON FIVERR" COVERS THE PRIMARY STEPS AND CRUCIAL STRATEGIES FOR BEGINNERS WHO WANT TO START THEIR FREELANCING CAREER ON THE PLATFORM. HERE IS AN OVERVIEW OF THIS TOPIC:

1. Account Setup: The process of getting started on Fiverr begins with creating an account. This involves providing some basic information such as your name, email, and password. Once you have submitted this information, you will receive an email with a verification link that you need to click on to verify your email address. After you have verified your email, you can set up your profile. This is an important step because it is the first impression that potential clients will have of you. You will need to provide information about your skills, expertise, and the services you are willing to offer. It is important to ensure your profile is well-written and highlights your strengths. Once you have set up your profile, you can start exploring the platform.

You can search for jobs that match your skills, or you can create gigs that showcase your services. When you find a job that you are interested in, you can submit a proposal to the client. If the client accepts your proposal, you can start working on the project. Overall, the process of getting started on Fiverr is easy to follow. By creating a strong profile and actively searching for jobs, you can start building your reputation on the platform and earning money for your skills and expertise.

2. Profile Optimization: To create an optimized profile, it is important to pay attention to some crucial details. Firstly, you should add a professional profile picture that gives off a positive and approachable vibe. Your picture should also be of high quality and resolution so that it doesn't appear pixelated or blurry. Secondly, writing a compelling bio that tells potential clients about your skills, experience, and expertise is key to making a good impression. It should be concise yet informative, highlighting your strengths and what sets you apart from others in your field. Lastly, showcasing relevant skills and experiences is essential to attract potential clients. This can be done by highlighting your past work experience, education, certifications, and any other relevant achievements that you want to showcase. By keeping these tips in mind, you can create an optimized profile that will help you stand out and attract more clients.

3. Understanding Fiverr Interface: For individuals who are new to a specific platform, it is highly recommended to invest time in learning the ins and outs of its navigation system, dashboard, and various tools available. These tools can include messaging, orders, analytics, and gig management. Becoming familiar with these features can be essential for beginners to effectively utilize the platform and optimize their experience.

Navigation System: The navigation system allows users to move through the platform and its various pages. It is essential to understand the layout of the platform to easily find the necessary features and tools.

Dashboard: The dashboard provides a centralized location for users to access important information and manage their account settings. It can display key performance metrics, such as earnings, ratings, and reviews.

Messaging: The messaging feature enables communication between users, such as clients and freelancers. Clear and timely communication is crucial for successful collaboration and project completion.

Orders: The orders feature allows clients to place orders for services and freelancers to manage and deliver those services. Understanding the order process is crucial for timely delivery and a positive client experience.

Analytics: Analytics provide insights into user performance, such as earnings, ratings, and reviews. Understanding analytics can help users track their progress and identify areas for improvement.

Gig Management: Gig management is the process of creating, managing, and delivering services on the platform. Freelancers need to understand how to properly manage their gigs to ensure timely delivery and a positive client experience.

Overall, investing time to become familiar with the platform's navigation system, dashboard, and various tools can help beginners effectively utilize the platform to its fullest potential.

4. Creating Engaging Gigs: As a newcomer to the world of gig creation, it's important to understand the key elements that make a gig stand out. To create a gig that catches the eye, you'll need to pay attention to several details. First and foremost, your title should be catchy, and engaging, and convey what your gig is all about. Next, be sure to provide a detailed description that accurately reflects what you offer and what sets you apart from the competition. Setting clear pricing is also crucial, as it helps potential buyers understand what they'll be getting for their money. Finally, high-quality images or samples can make all the difference, giving buyers a clear idea of what they can expect when they purchase your gig. By mastering these essential components, you'll be well on your way to creating gigs that truly stand out in the marketplace.

5. Selecting the Right Category: When it comes to creating a profile and offering services on a platform, selecting the appropriate category and subcategory is essential for effectively promoting one's skills and services. Categories and subcategories serve as a means of grouping and organizing services, and they play a critical role in helping potential clients discover and select the right service provider. To maximize visibility and attract potential clients, it is crucial to choose a category and subcategory that closely aligns with one's skills and services. This is because the platform's search algorithm primarily relies on categories and subcategories when matching clients with service providers.

To select the most appropriate category and subcategory, one should consider the specific nature of their services and the skills they possess. For example, if one offers web design services, one should select "Web, Mobile & Software Development" as the primary category and "Web & Mobile Design" as the subcategory. This way, they are more likely to be discovered by clients who are searching for web design services. Overall, selecting the right category and subcategory requires careful consideration and attention to detail. By taking the time to choose the appropriate categories, service providers can increase their visibility and attract more potential clients, ultimately leading to more successful projects and increased revenue.

6. Setting Realistic Goals: For beginners in any field, setting achievable goals is crucial for staying focused and motivated. In the gig economy, goals could be related to the number of gigs offered, the frequency of client interactions, or the amount of earnings generated. By setting specific, measurable, and realistic goals, beginners can track their progress, stay motivated, and celebrate their accomplishments. Whether it's aiming to secure a certain number of gigs per week or earning a specific amount of income per month, setting achievable goals can help beginners build momentum, improve their skills, and establish a successful career in the gig economy.

7. Utilizing Fiverr Resources:

For those who are just starting out in the freelancing world, Fiverr offers a wealth of resources to help you get started. By exploring Fiverr's guides, tutorials, and forums, you can gain valuable insights, tips, and best practices to jumpstart your freelancing career. These resources can provide you with the knowledge and tools you need to succeed in the competitive world of freelancing.

8. Initial Gig Promotion:

Are you looking to kickstart your gig and gain more visibility? One effective way to achieve this is by promoting your gigs through social media, networking, or by utilizing Fiverr's internal promotional tools. These methods can help you gain the initial traction you need to succeed. So, why not give them a try and see the difference they can make?

9. Pricing Strategies: For those who are new to running a business, it's important to grasp the concept of pricing strategies and how they can be used to your advantage. When you're first starting, it can be tempting to offer low prices to attract customers, but it's important to keep in mind that this can be unsustainable in the long term. Instead, you'll want to find a middle ground where you're offering competitive rates while still providing enough value to your clients that they'll be willing to pay for your services.

One popular pricing strategy is to offer a "freemium" model, where you offer a basic service for free and charge for additional features or premium services. This can be a great way to get customers in the door and build a relationship with them, while still generating revenue from those who are willing to pay for more.

Another strategy is to offer tiered pricing, where you offer different levels of service at different price points. This allows customers to choose the level of service that's right for them, while still allowing you to upsell them to higher tiers if they need more value.

Ultimately, the key is to find a pricing strategy that works for your business and your customers. By doing so, you'll be able to attract and retain customers while still generating the revenue you need to keep your business running smoothly.

10. Patience and Persistence: Establishing oneself on Fiverr as a service provider can be a challenging pursuit, requiring a combination of perseverance and patience. Gaining a reputation and building a clientele necessitates a consistent display of quality work, which is a fundamental factor in attaining success on the platform.

If you're new to Fiverr, it's important to learn how to get started properly. This will give you the tools and knowledge you need to use the platform effectively and start your freelance career on the right foot.

Fiverr freelancing has become an increasingly important aspect of many people's professional journeys and prospects. This platform offers a vast range of opportunities for individuals to showcase their skills, earn financial independence, and create multiple revenue streams. In addition to monetary benefits, Fiverr provides a global network that allows exposure to diverse projects, clients, and cultures, thereby refining communication and adaptability skills. By embracing freelancing on Fiverr, individuals can explore entrepreneurship, achieve work-life balance, and continually evolve in an ever-changing job landscape. In a rapidly evolving digital economy, Fiverr freelancing serves as a gateway for individuals to carve their paths, grow professionally, and adapt to the future of work.

BY ABDUL RAUF

SETTING UP YOUR FIVERR ACCOUNT

Setting up your Fiverr account is the first step towards establishing a successful freelance presence on the platform. The process is quite simple and begins with creating an account, where you will be asked to provide basic personal details such as your name, email, and password. You will also need to verify your email address before proceeding.

Once you have completed the account setup process, it's time to start building your profile. Your profile is like a digital portfolio that showcases your expertise, skills, and the services you offer. To make your profile stand out, you will need to add a professional profile picture, write a captivating bio that highlights your strengths, and emphasize your skills to attract potential clients.

Navigating Fiverr's dashboard is also an essential part of setting up your account. The dashboard is your central hub for managing your freelance business, where you can access features such as messaging, orders, analytics, and gig management. Messaging allows you to communicate with potential clients and collaborators, while orders let you track your ongoing projects. Analytics provides you with insights into your performance, such as the number of clicks and views on your profile, while gig management lets you create and manage your services.

In summary, setting up a Fiverr account is a straightforward process that requires you to create your profile and navigate the dashboard. By doing this, you will be well-equipped to succeed as a freelancer on the platform.

CRAFTING AN OPTIMIZED PROFILE

HERE ARE THE MAIN POINTS FOR CRAFTING AN OPTIMIZED PROFILE ON FIVERR:

1. Professional Profile Picture: When selecting a photo to represent yourself, it's important to choose one that is clear and professional-looking. This means that the photo should be of high quality, with good lighting and a clear focus on your face. You should also consider the background of the photo, making sure that it is not distracting or unprofessional. It's important to remember that the photo you choose will be a representation of you, so take the time to select one that you feel accurately reflects your personality and professionalism.

2. Compelling Bio: When writing in Plain English, it's important to consider the audience you are addressing. Different groups have different needs and require specific information. Therefore, it's crucial to organize the text logically by putting the most important information first. To avoid confusion, sentences should be short and only contain necessary information. Long, wordy sentences tend to overload the reader with too much information and detract from the main point. The text should be concise, direct, and easy to follow.

To ensure clarity, use simple and familiar vocabulary. Everyday language is preferred over acronyms, jargon, and legal terms. Plain English encourages the use of verbs instead of nouns. Additionally, using the active voice helps to make the text more easy to understand.

Remember not to change the meaning of the original text, add any new information, or remove important details. By following these guidelines, you can create a text in Plain English that is accessible to a wide audience.

3. Showcase Expertise: Please provide a comprehensive list of your skills, certifications, and unique qualities that make you stand out. This includes any technical expertise you may possess, any relevant industry certifications or qualifications you may have earned, and any personal qualities or soft skills that set you apart from others. For example, if you are a software developer, list the programming languages, frameworks, and tools you are proficient in. Similarly, if you have any recognized certifications like PMP, CCNA, or any other professional qualification, you should mention that as well. Lastly, highlight some of your personal qualities, such as excellent communication skills, adaptability, leadership, or creativity that make you an asset to any team or organization you work with.

4. Portfolio and Samples: When you're applying for a job or pitching a project, it's always a good idea to showcase your skills and expertise by providing samples of your previous work. This can give potential employers or clients a better sense of your capabilities, style, and approach. Whether you're a writer, designer, developer, or any other kind of professional, sharing your portfolio or examples of your work can help you stand out from the competition and demonstrate your value. So, be sure to gather your best samples, organize them in a clear and accessible way, and professionally present them.

5. Clear Service Description: To attract potential clients, it's important to define the services offered clearly and comprehensively. This means providing a detailed description of the services, including the specific benefits and outcomes that clients can expect. It's also important to highlight any unique features or advantages that set your services apart from others in the same industry. Additionally, pricing information and outlining guarantees or service-level agreements can help build trust and credibility with potential clients. Taking the time to clearly define your services can ultimately lead to higher conversion rates and increased customer satisfaction.

6. Keywords for Searchability: To improve the visibility of your services, it is important to incorporate relevant keywords that reflect your business offerings. These keywords should be carefully selected based on their popularity and relevance to your target audience.

By including such keywords in your website content, titles, and meta descriptions, you can increase the likelihood of attracting potential customers who are searching for services like yours on search engines. Additionally, using long-tail keywords that are more specific to your services can also help you rank higher in search results and attract more qualified leads.

7. Accurate Pricing: It is important to set prices for your products or services that are both competitive and reasonable. This means that you should consider the value that you are offering to your customers and ensure that your pricing is aligned with that value. By setting competitive prices, you can attract more customers and remain competitive in your industry. At the same time, it is important to ensure that your prices are reasonable and not too high, as this can turn potential customers away. Ultimately, finding the right balance between competitive pricing and reasonable pricing can help you achieve success in your business and maintain a loyal customer base.

8. Responsive Communication: To establish a healthy and trustworthy relationship with potential customers, it is crucial to communicate with them in a timely and respectful manner. This means that you should respond to their queries and concerns promptly, without keeping them waiting for long periods. Additionally, it is important to be respectful and courteous in your interactions and to avoid using any language or tone that might be considered rude or dismissive. By doing so, you can build a positive and lasting relationship with your customers, which can help to increase their loyalty and trust in your brand over time.

9. Regular Profile Updates: When it comes to building a successful relationship with potential customers, effective communication is key. It is important to prioritize timely and respectful communication to establish trust and credibility. This can include promptly responding to inquiries and addressing any concerns or questions that may arise. By actively engaging with potential customers and demonstrating your willingness to provide excellent customer service, you can foster a positive relationship that is built on trust and mutual respect.

10. Client Reviews and Ratings:

To ensure that your customers are satisfied with your work, it is vital to provide high-quality service that meets or exceeds their expectations. This can be achieved by paying attention to detail, being proactive in identifying and addressing any issues that arise, and always striving to improve your skills and knowledge. Additionally, it is important to communicate effectively with your customers, listen carefully to their concerns, and take their feedback seriously. By doing so, you can build a strong reputation for providing top-notch work and exceptional service, which can lead to positive reviews, repeat business, and new referrals.

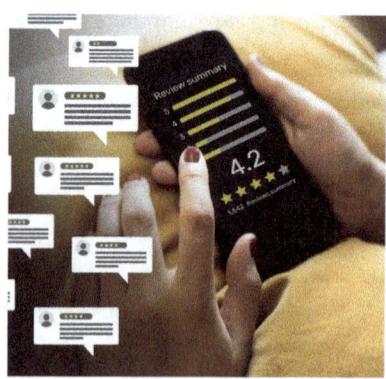

I truly believe that a clutter-free home can be a catalyst for positive change, and I'm eager to help others find the peace and contentment that comes with simple living.

– Abdul Rauf

UNDERSTANDING FIVERR'S PLATFORM AND FEATURES

If you're a freelancer looking for work, you might have heard of Fiverr. It's a website that connects freelancers with people who need different kinds of services. But, to be successful on Fiverr, you need to understand how it works. First, you need to know that Fiverr has many different features that can help you find work, communicate with clients, and manage your projects. When you sign up, you'll see a dashboard that lets you access all of these tools. One of the most important things you'll do on Fiverr is create "gigs." These are like ads for your services. You'll describe what you can do, how much you charge, and how long it will take. Clients can browse through gigs to find freelancers who can help them with their projects.

When you start working with a client, you'll need to talk to them a lot. Fiverr has a messaging system that makes it easy to communicate with clients. You'll use this to talk about the project, ask questions, and make sure everything is going smoothly. Fiverr also has tools that can help you understand how you're doing on the platform. For example, you can see how many people have looked at your gigs, how many people have clicked on them, and how many people have hired you. This can help you figure out what you're doing well and what you need to improve. Finally, Fiverr has two special features that might be helpful for you. Fiverr Pro is for freelancers who offer high-quality services. If you're accepted into Fiverr Pro, you'll be able to charge more money for your work. Fiverr Business is for people who need freelancers to help them with their business projects. If you're interested in working with businesses, you might want to check this out. By understanding how Fiverr works and using all of its features effectively, you can find more work, communicate better with clients, and improve your skills as a freelancer.

CHOOSING YOUR FREELANCE NICHE

HERE ARE THE MAIN POINTS ELABORATING ON "CHOOSING YOUR FREELANCE NICHE"

1. Self-Assessment: To identify areas where you excel and enjoy working, it's important to first assess your skills, passions, and expertise. Take a closer look at your professional background, hobbies, and interests, and consider how they can be translated into potential niches. Think about the specific skills you possess, such as writing, marketing, or design, and how they can be applied to different areas. Reflect on your passions, and ask yourself where you feel most fulfilled and engaged. Finally, consider your expertise and experience in certain fields, and how you can leverage them to create a unique niche in the market. By taking these factors into account, you can identify areas where you have a competitive advantage and a genuine interest, setting yourself up for success in your chosen field.

2. Market Research: If you're thinking about offering your services on Fiverr, it's important to do some research first. This means looking into what kind of services people are looking for, what other freelancers are offering, and what kinds of things clients typically require. By doing this, you'll be able to identify areas where you might be able to stand out and make some money.

3, Identify Unique Strengths:

- Use concrete examples to illustrate your unique skills, experiences, or specialized knowledge. This will make your writing more engaging and help potential clients better understand the value you can offer.

- Avoid using jargon or technical language that may be unclear to readers outside of your niche. Instead, use plain language and provide explanations or definitions when necessary.

- Consider including testimonials or case studies from past clients to provide social proof of your value and expertise. This can help potential clients feel more confident in their decision to work with you.

4. Passion and Proficiency: To achieve success in your chosen field, it's crucial to balance your passion with proficiency. This means finding a niche where your skills align with your interests, ensuring sustained motivation and a higher quality of work.

Choosing a niche that aligns with your skills means selecting a field where you possess the necessary expertise, qualifications, and experience. Your skills can include professional and technical abilities, such as programming, writing, accounting, or marketing, among others, that allow you to excel in your niche.

On the other hand, aligning your niche with your interests is equally important. It ensures that you enjoy what you do and are motivated to continue learning, growing, and innovating in your field. When you pursue a niche that aligns with your interests, you're more likely to be passionate about your work, which can translate into higher-quality output.

In short, balancing passion with proficiency is a recipe for success in any field. By choosing a niche where your skills and interests converge, you can ensure sustained motivation, high-quality work, and a fulfilling career.

5. Target Audience: It's important to define your target audience within your niche to effectively tailor your services and marketing efforts. To do this, you should conduct thorough research to understand their needs, pain points, and preferences. This will enable you to create more targeted and effective messaging that resonates with your audience. By understanding their needs and preferences, you can also adjust your services to better meet their requirements, ultimately leading to higher levels of customer satisfaction and retention. Therefore, it's crucial to invest time and effort in researching and understanding your target audience to ensure your business is meeting their needs effectively.

6. Evaluate Competition: When you're starting a business, it's essential to consider your competitors and the services they offer. Take the time to analyze their offerings and identify any gaps or opportunities that exist in your chosen niche. This will help you determine how you can provide unique or improved services to stand out from the competition. By doing so, you'll be better positioned to attract customers and build a successful business in your industry.

7. Scalability and Future Prospects: When considering a niche, it's important to assess its scalability and potential for future growth. This involves analyzing whether the niche allows for potential diversification and long-term sustainability in terms of demand and evolving market trends. It's important to look at the current state of the market and the direction it's headed to determine if the niche has the potential to adapt and thrive in the future. Additionally, it's important to consider if there are any barriers to entry or potential roadblocks that could hinder growth in the future. By doing a thorough assessment, you can identify whether a niche is worth pursuing and has the potential to lead to long-term success.

8. Testing and Iteration: To kickstart your business, it's best to begin by providing services within the specific niche you are an expert in. However, it's important to remember that the market is constantly evolving, and client feedback can be critical in shaping your offerings. It's essential to be open to testing and iterating your services, modifying them in response to feedback from clients and changes in market trends. As you continue to grow and gain more expertise, you can use this knowledge to refine your niche and develop services that are even more tailored to the needs of your clients.

9. Specialization vs. Versatility: When it comes to offering services, there are two broad approaches you can take: specializing in a narrow niche or offering a broader range of services. Specializing in a narrow niche means focusing on a specific area of expertise and offering services related to that area only. On the other hand, offering a broader range of services means catering to a wider range of client needs by offering services related to different areas of expertise.

While specializing in a narrow niche can help you establish yourself as an expert in a particular field, it may limit your client base. On the other hand, offering a broader range of services can help you cater to diverse client needs, but may dilute your expertise and make it harder for clients to perceive you as an expert in any one area.

Therefore, it is essential to find a balance that allows you to showcase your expertise while catering to diverse client needs. This might involve focusing on a specific area of expertise while offering related services or finding a way to package your services in a way that appeals to clients with diverse needs. By finding this balance, you can establish yourself as an expert in your field while still catering to the needs of a wide range of clients.

10. Commitment and Flexibility: When selecting a niche, it is crucial to commit to it fully. However, it is equally important to remain flexible and adaptable to change as needed. To be successful in your chosen niche, it is essential to continually refine your skills, stay up-to-date with the latest industry trends, and be open to exploring new opportunities that may arise within or adjacent to your niche. By doing so, you can position yourself as an expert in your field while also expanding your knowledge and skillset to stay ahead of the competition. Remember, commitment and flexibility are key to long-term success in any niche.

When setting up a profile or portfolio on a freelancing platform like Fiverr, it's crucial to include relevant screenshots of successful gigs, Fiverr dashboard analytics, and examples of quality work. These visuals offer concrete proof of your capabilities and help potential clients make informed decisions about hiring you. By showcasing past successes, performance metrics, and the high-quality services you provide, you can demonstrate your expertise, professionalism, and commitment to delivering exceptional results. The inclusion of visually impactful materials will further enhance your portfolio and help you stand out among other freelancers. Therefore, it's essential to carefully select and present your best work in a visually appealing manner, as this could be the deciding factor for potential clients when choosing a freelancer. By providing compelling evidence of your capabilities, you increase your chances of landing new projects and building a strong reputation as a skilled and reliable freelancer.

EXPLORING DIFFERENT FIVERR CATEGORIES

Fiverr is a widely popular online platform that offers an extensive range of services across numerous categories, making it an ideal hub for freelancers to showcase their skills and expertise. The platform boasts a vast and diverse spectrum of service categories spanning various industries and professions, including graphic design, writing and translation, digital marketing, programming, video and animation, music and audio, business services, and more. Each category encompasses subcategories, allowing freelancers to specialize in specific areas and offer services aligned with their skills and expertise.

Exploring different Fiverr categories is a crucial step for freelancers looking to succeed on the platform. By delving into the various categories, freelancers can identify their areas of specialization, understand the needs of their potential clients, and choose the categories that best match their skills and interests. This exploration aids freelancers in identifying niches that they can focus on, thus enhancing their visibility on the platform, increasing their chances of getting hired, and building a loyal client base.

For instance, the Graphic Design category on Fiverr includes subcategories like Logo Design, Brand Style Guides, Packaging Design, and many more. Similarly, the Writing and Translation category includes subcategories like Articles and blog Posts, Creative Writing, Translation, and more. By exploring these subcategories, freelancers can identify the areas they excel in and can specialize in the categories that match their expertise. This helps them to stand out from the competition and position themselves for success.

In conclusion, Fiverr's extensive range of categories and subcategories makes it an excellent platform for freelancers to showcase their skills and build their careers. By exploring and understanding the different categories and subcategories, freelancers can position themselves strategically for success and stand out from the competition. This results in a successful freelancing career that is built upon a strong foundation of expertise and specialization.

HERE ARE THE MAIN POINTS FOR "EXPLORING DIFFERENT FIVERR CATEGORIES"

1. Diverse Categories: Fiverr is an online platform that offers an extensive range of service categories. These categories span across diverse industries such as graphic design, writing, programming, marketing, and many more. Fiverr provides a vast pool of skilled professionals who are experts in their respective fields. This platform is a go-to destination for businesses and individuals looking to outsource work, find freelancers for their projects, or hire professionals for their specific needs.

2. Specialized Subcategories: Every industry has different types of jobs that require unique skills and expertise. To make it easier to navigate through the various job roles, each category is further divided into specialized subcategories. These subcategories are designed to cater to specific skills or services within the industry. By breaking down the broader industry into smaller categories, it becomes easier for individuals to identify job opportunities that match their skills and interests.

3. Exploration Opportunity: As a freelancer, you have the freedom to choose from a wide range of categories that match your skill set, interests, and specialized knowledge. By exploring these different categories, you can identify the most suitable areas for you to showcase your expertise and stand out in the market.

4. Understanding Client Needs: By exploring different categories, freelancers can gain a better understanding of what clients are looking for. This helps them to customize their services to meet specific demands and requirements. By doing so, freelancers can increase their chances of attracting clients and delivering high-quality work that meets their needs and expectations.

5. Niche Identification: Exploring different areas of expertise can help freelancers identify their niche and create a specialized space catering to their unique strengths. This process can be incredibly helpful in distinguishing oneself from competitors and building a successful freelance career.

6. Portfolio Development: One of the keys to creating a successful portfolio is to choose categories that are relevant to your expertise. By focusing on specific areas, you can demonstrate your knowledge and experience in those fields, which can help you stand out from the competition. For example, if you specialize in digital marketing, you might choose categories like social media marketing, email marketing, and search engine optimization to showcase your skills. By doing so, you can target clients who are specifically looking for those services, which can lead to more business opportunities. Additionally, focusing on specific categories can help you develop a more focused and refined portfolio, which can make it easier for potential clients to understand what you have to offer.

7. Competition Analysis: To delve into different categories, one must conduct a thorough analysis of the competition within each of them. This helps freelancers in comprehending the existing market demand and the levels of competition they are likely to face in their respective fields. By exploring the categories in detail, freelancers can gain valuable insights and make informed decisions about their career paths.

8. Adaptability and Growth: This statement emphasizes the importance of being adaptable and open to exploring new areas of interest. It suggests that as an individual's skills and knowledge evolve, they could potentially expand their horizons by exploring new categories or subcategories of their field. This approach may open up new opportunities for growth and development, both personally and professionally. It highlights the importance of staying curious, experimenting with new ideas, and being willing to step out of one's comfort zone to pursue new avenues of learning and growth.

9. Alignment with Skills: For people who work independently, it's important to find work that they enjoy and are good at. By focusing on the things they're passionate about and skilled in, they can stay motivated and produce high-quality work.

10. Strategic Decision Making: Having a clear understanding of the different categories is crucial for individuals or businesses looking to offer services or products in the market. By categorizing products or services based on their features and attributes, it becomes easier to identify the target audience and tailor one's offerings accordingly. Categorization also helps in positioning oneself in the market by identifying the competition and differentiating one's services or products from others in the same category. It enables businesses to make informed decisions about marketing, pricing, and branding strategies to attract and retain customers effectively. Therefore, understanding different categories is an essential aspect of market research that can impact the success of any business.

FINDING YOUR EXPERTISE AND PASSION

HERE ARE THE MAIN POINTS FOR "FINDING YOUR EXPERTISE AND PASSION":

1. Self-Reflection: If you're looking to gain a deeper understanding of your skills, experiences, and interests, it's important to take a thorough and introspective approach. Start by taking a step back and examining the tasks and activities that you have excelled in throughout your life. Look for the underlying patterns and common themes that emerge, and try to understand what specific skills and strengths you possess that enable you to perform well in these areas. Additionally, consider reflecting on the experiences that have brought you the most joy and fulfillment. Perhaps there are certain activities or hobbies that you've always been drawn to, or certain types of problems that you find particularly intriguing. Pay attention to these inclinations, as they can be powerful indicators of your passions and interests.

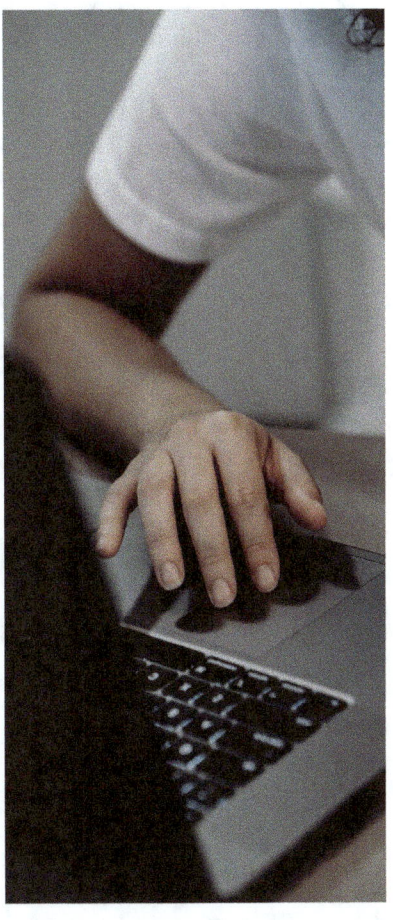

By taking a holistic and thoughtful approach to self-reflection, you can gain a deeper understanding of yourself and the unique strengths and passions that you possess. Armed with this knowledge, you'll be better equipped to pursue a career or other pursuits that align with your values and bring you a sense of purpose and fulfillment.

2. Assessing Strengths: It's always a good idea to take a moment and evaluate your strengths and unique talents, especially when it comes to a particular field or skill set you are interested in. This can involve listing specific skills, experiences, or knowledge that sets you apart from others in the same field. By doing so, you can better understand your unique value proposition and leverage it to achieve your goals. It's also important to continuously develop and refine your strengths to stay competitive and relevant in your chosen field.

3. Exploring Interests: One way to find a career that you truly enjoy is to explore different fields or industries. By trying out various jobs, you can discover what makes you feel passionate and enthusiastic. Take the time to reflect on what you enjoy and what you're good at, and use this information to guide your search. When you find a job that resonates with your passions, you'll be more motivated and fulfilled in your work.

4. Trial and Error: How about this? "Why stick with the same old routine when you can experiment with new tasks and projects? It's a great way to discover your interests and skills and figure out what you enjoy doing most. So go ahead, give it a try, and see where it takes you!"

5. Feedback and Self-Assessment: It's important to actively seek feedback from those around you and take a critical look at your performance. This will allow you to hone in on your areas of expertise and continue to improve upon them.

6. Identifying Market Demand: If you are thinking about starting a freelance career, it's important to identify the skills or services that are in high demand in the market. You can then match those skills or services with your interests and passions to create a successful and fulfilling freelance career.

7. Research and Learning: To ensure that you are well informed and equipped to meet the needs of the ever-changing market, it is imperative that you make a consistent effort to research and learn about new industries and skills. By staying up-to-date on emerging trends and technologies, you can keep your knowledge and expertise aligned with the current market demand, making you a valuable asset in your field.

8. Networking and Exposure: To gain a better understanding of potential niches that align with your interests, it can be incredibly helpful to engage with communities, mentors, or professionals in those areas. By participating in discussions and activities related to your interests, you can gain valuable exposure to the latest trends and developments in those fields. Additionally, seeking out guidance from experienced mentors and professionals can provide you with valuable insights and advice on how best to navigate your chosen industry. Whether it's attending networking events, joining online forums, or simply reaching out to individuals who share your passion, actively seeking out opportunities to engage with others in your areas of interest can be a great way to expand your knowledge and build meaningful connections.

9. Flexibility and Adaptability: In today's rapidly changing world, it is important to remain open to exploring new opportunities and keep upgrading your skills to stay relevant. As technology advances and new trends emerge, it is crucial to adapt and evolve your expertise to meet the changing demands of the industry. Being proactive and open to learning new things can help you stay ahead of the curve and make the most of the opportunities that come your way. So, keep an eye on the latest developments in your field and be ready to embrace change to succeed in your career.

10. Passion-Proficiency Balance: To be successful in any field, it is important to find the perfect balance between your passions and your proficiency. This means identifying areas where your skills and enthusiasm intersect and then putting in the effort to develop those areas further. To achieve this, it is essential to take the time to explore your interests and discover what truly motivates you. Once you have identified your passions, you can begin honing your skills and knowledge in those areas, while also seeking out new opportunities to learn and grow. Finding this equilibrium requires both self-awareness and a willingness to take risks. You may need to step out of your comfort zone and try new things to discover what truly inspires you. You may also need to invest time and effort in developing new skills or refining existing ones. But, with persistence and dedication, you can achieve great things. Success is not only about reaching your goals but also enjoying the journey.

NAVIGATING MARKET DEMAND AND TRENDS

HERE ARE FIVE COMPREHENSIVE MAIN POINTS FOR "NAVIGATING MARKET DEMAND AND TRENDS"

1. Thorough Market Research: To gain a comprehensive understanding of the current market demand and identify emerging trends within your industry or niche, it is essential to conduct thorough and meticulous research. This process requires the use of various analytical tools, such as Google Analytics, SEMrush, and Ahrefs, to collect and analyze data and insights on client preferences, popular services, and industry trends. Keyword research is another indispensable aspect of this process, as it enables you to identify and target relevant keywords and phrases that are driving traffic to your website or your competitors' websites. Furthermore, trend analysis is a powerful tool that can help you recognize emerging patterns and changes in consumer behavior, allowing you to remain agile and adaptable in the face of shifting market forces. By staying up-to-date on market demand and emerging trends, you can make well-informed, data-driven decisions that will aid you in growing your business and achieving success.

2. Client Needs Analysis: To provide the best possible service to your clients, it's important to pay close attention to their requests, feedback, and reviews. By analyzing this information, you can gain valuable insights into their specific needs and preferences, allowing you to tailor your services to meet their expectations. Additionally, keeping a close eye on the types of services that are in high demand can help you stay ahead of the curve and ensure that your offerings remain relevant and appealing to your clients. By staying attuned to your client's needs and staying up-to-date on industry trends, you can position yourself as a reliable and trusted provider of the services your clients require.

3. Stay Updated with Industry Trends: To stay up-to-date with the latest trends and developments in your industry, it's important to make a habit of regularly reading industry publications, participating in forums, and following authoritative blogs. By doing so, you'll gain valuable insights into the latest technological advancements, shifting client expectations, and emerging market trends. This knowledge can help you make informed decisions and stay ahead of the competition. Additionally, staying informed about developments in your industry can help you identify emerging opportunities, potential threats, and areas for growth. So don't neglect this important aspect of professional development, and make sure to keep abreast of the latest news and trends in your field.

4. Networking and Engagement: To stay ahead in the game, it's crucial to engage with industry peers, experts, and potential clients. This helps you gain valuable insights into their evolving needs and upcoming trends. One of the best ways to do this is by participating in relevant communities or events that cater to your niche. By doing so, you can expand your network, build meaningful relationships, and gather market intelligence that can inform your business decisions. Attending conferences, meetups, seminars, and webinars can also help you stay updated on the latest developments in your industry and keep you abreast of emerging technologies and best practices. Additionally, joining online forums, social media groups, and professional associations can help you connect with like-minded individuals and foster collaborations that can boost your business growth. So, make sure to allocate enough time and resources to engage with your industry peers and clients, and stay on top of the game.

5. Adaptability and Skill Enhancement: In today's fast-changing business landscape, it's important to stay ahead of the curve by continuously refining and adapting your skill sets. This means keeping a close eye on emerging trends and client demands and being willing to adjust your approach accordingly. To stay competitive, you need to stay flexible in your approach, be open to learning new skills and technologies, and proactively position yourself to meet evolving market needs. This might involve taking courses or attending workshops to acquire new knowledge and skills, networking with industry peers to stay up-to-date on the latest developments, and seeking out opportunities to apply your skills in new and innovative ways. By staying proactive and adaptable, you can ensure that you remain a valuable asset to your clients and colleagues, and that you are always well-positioned to thrive in today's dynamic business environment.

Adaptability skills are essential for individuals to thrive in dynamic environments. With the ability to swiftly adjust to changes, one can build resilience and be well-equipped to tackle any challenge that comes their way.

CREATING COMPELLING GIGS

HERE ARE SEVEN DETAILED MAIN POINTS FOR "CREATING COMPELLING GIGS"

1. Identifying Client Needs: To begin with, it is important to conduct thorough research and gain a deep understanding of the specific needs and preferences of potential clients within your niche. This involves analyzing various aspects such as existing gigs, client requests, and market trends. By doing so, you can discern what services are in demand and tailor your offerings accordingly to attract more clients. It is also essential to keep track of any changes in the market and adapt your services as needed to stay ahead of the competition. By staying up-to-date and consistently delivering high-quality services, you can establish a solid reputation and build a loyal client base.

2. Clear and Detailed Descriptions: When creating gig titles and descriptions, it is important to find a balance between being concise and comprehensive. You should communicate your services clearly while also highlighting the value you can offer to clients and how your services can help solve their problems or fulfill their needs. This requires choosing your words carefully and presenting your information with intention. You may want to emphasize your unique skills, experience, or selling points which sets you apart from other freelancers. In addition, showcasing your portfolio or past work is a great way to give potential clients an idea of your capabilities. Ultimately, a well-crafted gig title and description can significantly increase your chances of attracting the right clients and securing more work opportunities.

3. Highlight Unique Selling Proposition (USP): When advertising your services, it's important to focus on what sets them apart from others in the marketplace. Highlight your unique skills, expertise, and approach to showcase why potential clients should choose your gig. Consider what distinguishes you from your competition and think about how you can emphasize those strengths to attract clients. By doing this, you can increase your chances of being selected for a job as clients are more likely to choose a service provider who offers something different and valuable. Therefore, take the time to identify what makes your services unique and ensure that you communicate it clearly in your marketing materials.

4. Eye-catching Visuals: When creating a gig, it's important to incorporate high-quality images, videos, or samples showcasing your previous work or the outcome clients can expect. Visuals are a powerful tool to increase the credibility and attractiveness of your gig, and they draw attention from potential clients. By including relevant and engaging visuals, you can demonstrate your skills and expertise, and give clients a better idea of what they can expect from your services. Make sure the visuals are of high quality and accurately represent your work, as this can greatly influence a client's decision to choose you over other sellers.

5. Optimized Pricing and Packages: Including high-quality images, videos, or samples that exhibit your previous work or what clients can expect as a result of your services is an excellent way to enhance the overall credibility and attractiveness of your gig. By showcasing your talent and expertise through visuals, you can effectively grab the attention of potential clients, increase their interest, and persuade them to choose your services over others. So, make sure to include visually appealing content in your gig to leave a long-lasting impression on your clients and to improve your chances of getting hired.

6. Call-to-Action (CTA): To attract more clients to your gig, it's important to create a compelling description that includes a strong and clear call-to-action. This should guide potential clients on what steps to take next and encourage them to engage with you. You could suggest messaging you for more information, placing an order, or contacting you to discuss their requirements in detail. By doing this, you'll make it easier for clients to take action and connect with you, which could lead to more sales and a better reputation on the platform.

7. Regular Updates and Optimization: It's important to keep improving your gigs to make sure they perform well and get noticed by potential customers. You can do this by trying out different ways of describing your gig, using eye-catching visuals, or changing the price to attract more buyers. Keep up with what's popular and what people are looking for, so you can adjust your gigs accordingly. By making these changes, you can increase your chances of success and stand out from the competition.

To create a gig that will grab the attention of potential clients, it is crucial to have a thorough understanding of their needs. You can achieve this by conducting market research, segmenting your audience, and analyzing their behaviors and preferences. In addition, effective communication is the key to conveying your value proposition, benefits, and unique selling points. It's also important to differentiate yourself from competitors by offering a unique angle, a fresh perspective, or a special skill set that sets you apart. Visual appeal is another crucial element to consider, as it can make your gig stand out from the crowd and attract more clicks and engagement. Finally, adaptability is essential to stay relevant and flexible in a fast-changing environment and adjust your gig according to feedback, market trends, and client demands. By mastering these key elements, you can create a compelling gig that resonates with potential clients and drives your success.

WRITING GIG DESCRIPTIONS THAT SELL

HERE ARE FIVE COMPREHENSIVE POINTS FOR "WRITING GIG DESCRIPTIONS THAT SELL"

1. Client-Centric Approach: When crafting gig descriptions, it is crucial to keep the client's needs in mind and focus on how your services can address their problems or fulfill their requirements. By outlining the value that clients will receive, you can highlight the benefits and solutions that are tailored to their specific concerns. This approach helps clients understand how your services can benefit them and encourages them to choose your gig over others. So, it's essential to create gig descriptions that are both informative and persuasive, highlighting the value you offer and demonstrating how your services can meet the client's needs.

2. Compelling Storytelling: Utilizing the power of storytelling in your descriptions is crucial for effectively engaging with clients. By sharing specific and compelling anecdotes, successes, or scenarios that resonate with your clients, you can provide them with a glimpse into the impact your services can have on their lives. For example, you can describe a previous client's experience with your services, highlighting the positive outcomes they achieved and how it transformed their lives for the better. This approach can enable clients to relate to your services on a more personal level, allowing them to recognize the value in what you offer. Through the effective use of storytelling, you can establish a connection with your clients that promotes trust and encourages them to select your services above others.

3. Detailed and Specific Offerings: When you're trying to explain your services, it's important to be very clear and explain everything in detail. That means you need to tell your clients exactly what they can expect when they work with you. This includes explaining the type of work you'll be doing, what makes your services special, and what you'll provide when you're finished. This will help your clients understand what they're paying for and make sure that everyone is on the same page right from the beginning. When you talk about the type of work you'll be doing, it's a good idea to explain everything in detail. This could include giving a timeline of when you'll be working on their project and what specific tasks you'll be doing.

It's also important to explain what makes your services unique. Maybe you have a special way of doing things or you have a lot of experience in a particular area. Whatever it is, make sure you let your clients know what sets you apart from other businesses that offer similar services. Finally, it's important to explain what your clients can expect when you're finished. This could be a report, a presentation, or some other kind of output that shows the value of your services. By taking the time to explain all of these things, you'll be able to build strong relationships with your clients that will last for a long time.

4. Keyword Optimization: Crafting a gig description that catches the attention of potential clients is a crucial step you need to take. However, it's not enough to just stuff your description with keywords. To make it effective, you need to use these keywords in a natural, conversational style that fits your overall tone. By including keywords that clients are likely to search for, you can improve your gig's visibility, which can lead to more clicks, views, and ultimately, more sales. However, choosing the right keywords is not a one-size-fits-all approach. You need to conduct some research to know what keywords your target audience is using to look for services like yours. This way, you can customize your gig description to match the language and terminology that your potential clients are using. A well-crafted gig description with relevant keywords not only helps clients find your services more easily, but it also portrays you as an expert in your field and can help you stand out from the competition.

5. Visual and Formatting Enhancements: To make your work more impressive and engaging, it's a great idea to incorporate various forms of visuals to complement your descriptions. This can include images, videos, samples, or any other appropriate visual aids. By doing so, you can provide your audience with a more comprehensive understanding of your work and make it more visually appealing. Additionally, formatting techniques such as bullet points or bold text can be used to break down complicated information into easily digestible chunks, making it easier for your audience to comprehend your message. This can also enhance the readability and attractiveness of your work, making it more likely to be well-received.

Conclusion: Creating gig descriptions that are highly effective in generating sales requires a comprehensive approach that addresses the specific needs of potential clients. The process begins with conducting thorough research to identify the unique requirements of potential clients, such as their pain points, preferences, and expectations. This information is then used to tailor the content of gig descriptions to meet those requirements. One effective technique for crafting gig descriptions that sell is to use storytelling. This involves creating a narrative that connects with clients emotionally, making them more likely to engage with the content. By using relatable examples and anecdotes, businesses can create a sense of empathy and build trust with potential clients. Another important aspect of creating effective gig descriptions is to provide clear and detailed information that addresses client needs. This includes outlining the benefits of the service, specific deliverables, timelines, and any other relevant details that the client may need to make an informed decision. Optimizing gig descriptions for search visibility is also crucial. This involves the use of relevant keywords that are likely to be used by potential clients when searching for the service. By including these keywords in strategic locations, such as the title and body of the description, businesses can increase the visibility of their gig descriptions in search results. Finally, enhancing readability through the use of visuals and formatting can greatly improve the effectiveness of gig descriptions. This includes the use of headings, bullet points, and images to break up the text and make it easier to read. By creating a visually appealing and easy-to-read gig description, businesses can compel potential clients to take action and ultimately increase sales.

DESIGNING EYE-CATCHING GIG IMAGES

HERE ARE FIVE DETAILED MAIN POINTS FOR "DESIGNING EYE-CATCHING GIG IMAGES"

1. **Visual Impact:** It's important to keep in mind that the images you select for your gig are the very first impression potential clients will have of your services. This means it's crucial to make them visually compelling and engaging, so you can immediately capture their interest and draw them in. By creating images that effectively communicate the value of your services in a clear and impactful way, you can inspire potential clients to take action and learn more about what you have to offer. Remember, your gig images are the first opportunity to make a great impression and start building a strong relationship with your clients. Therefore, it's important to ensure that the images you choose are of high quality, eye-catching, and relevant to the services you are offering. You can also consider adding text overlays or other design elements to further enhance the visual appeal and convey the benefits of your services. By taking the time to create compelling gig images, you can set yourself apart from the competition and establish yourself as a trusted and reliable service provider.

2. **Relevance and Clarity:** When creating your gig, it's crucial to choose images that accurately represent the services you offer. These images should provide clients with a clear and concise idea of what they can expect from your services. For instance, if you're offering web design services, you should include images of websites you've designed in the past as well as screenshots of the design process. Additionally, it's essential to emphasize any unique service offerings that you have. You can do this by including images of unique features that you offer, such as custom graphics or specialized software. By showcasing these unique aspects of your services, you can help clients understand what sets you apart from others in your field. Keep in mind that the images you choose should not only be relevant to your services but also visually appealing. Ensure that they're high-quality and eye-catching, as this can help to attract the attention of potential clients.

3. Consistent Branding: To establish an easily recognizable brand, it is essential to maintain a consistent visual identity across all gig images. This can be achieved by employing consistent colors, fonts, and design elements that are aligned with your overall branding strategy. This means that all gig images should use the same color scheme, typography, and visual elements that your brand uses across all of its marketing materials, including your website, social media, and other promotional materials. Consistency in visual identity is crucial when it comes to building a strong brand image. By using the same design elements and color palette across all of your gig images, you can create a cohesive and memorable brand experience for your audience. This will help you stand out from your competitors and establish a strong brand identity that people can easily recognize.

In addition to distinguishing your brand from others, consistency in visual identity can also help build trust and credibility with your audience. It conveys a sense of professionalism and attention to detail, which can make your brand appear more trustworthy and reliable. So, if you want to create a strong brand image and build a loyal following, it is essential to maintain a consistent visual identity across all of your gig images.

4. Professional Quality: When it comes to creating visuals for your brand, the quality of your images plays a crucial role in establishing credibility and professionalism in the eyes of your target audience. Therefore, it is essential to pay attention to every little detail when designing your visuals. One of the key aspects is using sharp graphics that are visually appealing and easy on the eye. High-resolution images are also important to ensure that the images are clear and crisp, even when viewed on large screens. In addition to the technical aspect, it is crucial to incorporate polished design elements that complement your overall branding strategy. This includes the use of color schemes, typography, and other visual elements that help convey your brand's message and values. By ensuring that your images are consistent with your branding strategy, you can establish a strong visual identity that resonates with your audience and builds trust. Whether you are creating images for your website, social media channels, or marketing materials, it is crucial to prioritize quality over quantity.

5. Iterative Testing: To create gig images that are both impactful and engaging to clients, it is important to experiment with a variety of different design elements, layouts, and visuals in order to determine the most effective approach. This can involve trying out different combinations of colors, fonts, images, and other visual elements to see what resonates most with your target audience. In addition to experimenting with different design elements, it is equally important to analyze performance metrics and audience feedback in order to refine and optimize your gig images for maximum impact. This can involve tracking key performance indicators such as click-through rates, conversion rates, and engagement rates to see how your audience is responding to your images. Based on this feedback, you can then make data-driven decisions about how to adjust your images to better engage your clients. For example, you may find that certain colors or images are more effective at capturing their attention, or that certain layouts or design elements are more effective at communicating your message. By continuously refining and optimizing your gig images based on these insights, you can achieve better results and increase client engagement over time.

SETTING COMPETITIVE PRICES AND PACKAGES

HERE ARE FIVE DETAILED MAIN POINTS FOR "SETTING COMPETITIVE PRICES AND PACKAGES"

1. Market Research and Analysis: To determine the most appropriate pricing strategy for your business, it is necessary to conduct comprehensive research within your niche. This research should aim to provide a clear understanding of prevailing rates and pricing strategies in your industry. One crucial factor to consider is competitor pricing. Analyze their pricing to gain insight into what clients are willing to pay for similar products or services in the market. Additionally, research industry standards and client expectations to get a clear picture of what clients are looking for and what prices they expect. By analyzing all these factors, you can gain a better understanding of the market landscape and develop a pricing strategy that is fair, competitive, and profitable for your business.

2. Value-Based Pricing: When it comes to setting prices for your services, it's important to think about the value you provide to your customers rather than just looking at what your competitors charge. You should focus on what makes your services special and how they can help your customers succeed. By doing this, you can justify your rates and make a difference in the market. Consider how your services can help your customers save time, and money, or make more money. Think about the unique skills and expertise that you bring to the table and how they can benefit your customers in ways your competition cannot. By highlighting these advantages, you can make it clear to potential customers why they should choose your services over others. Additionally, make sure to communicate the value of your services effectively in all your marketing materials. Use examples and testimonials to show how your services have helped other customers achieve their goals. By doing this, you can build trust and credibility with potential customers, and make it easier for them to see the value in what you offer. In summary, by pricing your services based on the value you provide rather than only looking at what your competitors charge, you can stand out in the market and attract the right customers.

3. Tiered Packages and Options: One way to cater to the diverse needs of clients is by offering tiered packages or pricing options. This approach allows clients to choose the package that best fits their needs and budget. To make this approach effective, it is important to present clear distinctions between packages, outlining the specific services, additional features, or levels of customization for each tier. This will help clients make informed decisions and ensure that they are getting the most value out of their investment. Additionally, it is important to consider the needs of different client segments and create packages that cater to those specific needs. By doing so, you can attract a wider range of clients and establish yourself as a provider that can meet the unique needs of each client.

4. Balancing Pricing and Profitability: Are you struggling to find the perfect pricing for your business? It's essential to strike a balance between being competitive and maintaining profitability. I know it's not an easy task, but don't worry, I've got your back! Let's work together to ensure that your rates cover your expenses, time invested, and desired profit margins while still being appealing to potential clients. With the right pricing strategy, you can take your business to the next level and attract more customers. Let's get started!

5. Flexibility and Adaptability: It's essential to stay adaptable with your pricing strategy. This means keeping an eye on what other businesses charge, listening to what your customers say, and paying attention to changes in the market. By doing this, you can make adjustments to your prices and packages to stay competitive. To start, look at what other companies charge for similar services to get an idea of what's reasonable. Then, listen to your customers to see if they have any complaints or suggestions about your prices or packages. This feedback can help you make changes to stay competitive. Finally, keep an eye on how many people want your services. If lots of people want what you offer, you might be able to charge more. But if not many people want it, you might need to lower your prices or offer discounts to stay competitive. By staying flexible with your prices, you can make sure your business stays strong and your customers stay happy.

BUILDING YOUR FIVERR BRAND

"Building Your Fiverr Brand" is a comprehensive guide that outlines the essential elements necessary for establishing a recognizable brand presence on the Fiverr platform. This chapter delves into the foundational aspects of brand creation, emphasizing the need for consistency across visual elements, messaging, and interactions. Furthermore, it explores differentiation strategies, encouraging freelancers to highlight their unique selling propositions, niche expertise, and specialized skills. The guide also sheds light on the significance of managing and leveraging client feedback, reviews, and experiences to enhance brand reputation. Additionally, it touches upon expanding brand reach, engaging with a broader audience, and maximizing brand influence to attract more clients and opportunities within the Fiverr marketplace. In essence, "Building Your Fiverr Brand" serves as a holistic guide for freelancers to establish a strong, trustworthy, and recognizable brand identity on Fiverr. By following the principles outlined in this guide, freelancers can create a brand that resonates with their audience, builds credibility, and opens doors to new opportunities within the freelance realm.

ESTABLISHING CREDIBILITY AND TRUST

HERE ARE THE MAIN POINTS FOR "ESTABLISHING CREDIBILITY AND TRUST"

Consistent High-Quality Service: Delivering high-quality work is crucial for building a loyal client base. It is important to ensure that every piece of work you deliver meets or exceeds client expectations. Consistency is key, as it fosters confidence and reliability in your work. Make sure that you take the time to review your work and double-check for errors or inconsistencies before submitting it to the client.

Professionalism and Communication: Maintaining professionalism in all interactions with clients is essential for building trust. Responding promptly to messages and adhering to deadlines shows that you take the client's needs seriously. Clear and respectful communication is crucial, as it helps avoid misunderstandings and ensures that the client is satisfied with your work.

Transparency and Clarity: It is important to clearly outline your services, pricing, and deliverables to avoid misunderstandings. Be transparent with your clients about what they can expect from you and what you will deliver to them. Make sure that you are clear about pricing and any additional costs that may arise. This will help build client confidence and trust in your work.

Positive Client Reviews: Encouraging and collecting positive client reviews and testimonials is important for building a positive reputation on the platform. Positive reviews help to showcase your skills, work ethic, and the quality of your work. They also make it easier for potential clients to find and trust you.

Complete and Professional Profile: Your profile is your first impression to potential clients. It is important to make sure that your profile is complete and professional. This includes showcasing your relevant skills, experience, and successes, as well as any relevant certifications or qualifications. This will help instill trust in potential clients and make it easier for you to secure work.

SHOWCASING YOUR PORTFOLIO AND SAMPLES

HERE ARE THE MAIN POINTS FOR "SHOWCASING YOUR PORTFOLIO AND SAMPLES"

Selective Display: Your portfolio is a crucial tool to showcase your skills and experience to potential clients. Therefore, it is essential to curate a portfolio that highlights your best work while displaying a diverse range of your skills and services. You should aim to choose samples that demonstrate your versatility across different styles or services you excel in.

Quality Over Quantity: While it may be tempting to include every project you have worked on, prioritizing quality over quantity is crucial. You must choose high-quality samples that best represent your expertise and abilities. This will help you create a strong impression on potential clients and demonstrate your attention to detail and professionalism.

Contextual Descriptions: Your portfolio should include a concise description for each sample. These descriptions should provide context, and explain project objectives, your role, and achieved outcomes. This will help potential clients understand the scope of your work and see how you have helped previous clients achieve their goals.

Regular Updates: Your portfolio is a living document that should be updated regularly to reflect your current abilities and recent projects. You should aim to add fresh samples or replace outdated ones to keep your portfolio up-to-date. This will help you stay relevant in a dynamic industry and showcase your latest skills and achievements.

Visual Representation: Your portfolio should be a visual representation of your skills and experience. You must choose samples that showcase your proficiency and versatility. You should also pay attention to the design and layout of your portfolio to ensure it looks professional and visually appealing. By doing so, you will create a strong impression on potential clients and increase your chances of getting hired.

UNDERSTANDING BUYER PSYCHOLOGY AND NEEDS

HERE ARE 10 DETAILED POINTS ON "UNDERSTANDING BUYER PSYCHOLOGY AND NEEDS"

Consumer Behavior Analysis: Gain insight into consumer behavior theories by understanding the decision-making processes, motivations, and triggers that influence purchasing choices. Emotional Triggers: Examine how emotions drive buyer decisions and acknowledge the significance of emotional connections, aspirations, fears, and desires in influencing purchase intentions.

Problem-Solution Dynamics: Gain an understanding of how buyers seek solutions to their problems or needs. Identify their pain points, challenges, and the specific solutions they seek. Value Perception: Analyze how buyers perceive value and the factors that influence their perception, such as quality, price, and the benefits they expect from a service or product.

Market Segmentation: Explore different buyer segments within your niche and identify their distinct needs, preferences, and behaviors to tailor your services accordingly. Decision-Making Models: Study decision-making models like the consumer decision process or decision-making matrices to comprehend buyer journeys and their thought processes.

Trust and Credibility: Investigate how trust and credibility impact buyer decisions and recognize the importance of positive reviews, testimonials, and a reputable brand image.

Cultural and Social Influences: Consider the cultural, social, and societal influences affecting buyer choices. Understand how cultural norms, trends, and social influences shape their decisions.

Brand Perception: Evaluate how buyers perceive brands and analyze the impact of brand loyalty, brand association, and brand image on their choices. Anticipating Future Needs: Stay ahead of the curve by anticipating evolving buyer needs and trends. Adapt your services to meet future demands while predicting market shifts and buyer expectations.

Anticipating Future Needs: Stay ahead of the curve by anticipating evolving buyer needs and trends. Adapt your services to meet future demands while predicting market shifts and buyer expectations.

To understand buyer psychology, we need to examine the various factors that influence purchasing decisions, such as emotional triggers, cognitive processes, problem-solving dynamics, value perceptions, and cultural and social influences on buyer behavior. By acknowledging these complexities, businesses can tailor their services to meet the unique needs and expectations of buyers, resulting in a more satisfying and rewarding buying experience.

MANAGING CLIENT RELATIONSHIPS

"Managing Client Relationships" is all about building and maintaining strong connections with clients. It means keeping in touch with them regularly, understanding what they need, and providing top-notch service. To be successful, it's important to listen carefully to clients and make sure you're on the same page with their goals. You also need to be honest and keep them informed throughout the process. Managing expectations is a crucial part of client management. That means being clear about what you can deliver and when. But you also need to be flexible and willing to adjust to their changing needs. If there are any problems or concerns, it's important to handle them professionally and quickly. And of course, delivering high-quality work is key to keeping clients happy and satisfied. It's also helpful to ask for feedback and suggestions for improvement. By doing this, you show clients that you care about their success and are committed to building a long-term relationship. Overall, managing client relationships is about clear communication, flexibility, delivering quality work, and building trust.

EFFECTIVE COMMUNICATION STRATEGIES

Active Listening: When dealing with clients, it is crucial to focus on attentive and empathetic listening. This means actively paying attention to what the client is saying, without interrupting them or letting distractions divert your attention. Additionally, empathetic listening involves understanding the client's needs, concerns, and objectives. It is important to put yourself in their shoes and try to see things from their perspective to provide the best possible service. By doing so, you can build trust and rapport with the client, which can be crucial in maintaining a positive and productive working relationship.

Clarity and Conciseness: When communicating with others, it's important to be clear and concise in your language to avoid confusion and misunderstandings. It's best to use simple words and avoid using industry jargon or technical terms that may not be familiar to the other person. Additionally, try to avoid using ambiguous language, which may have different meanings to different people. By using clear and concise language, you can ensure mutual understanding and effective communication.

Timely and Regular Updates: To maintain transparency and ensure that all stakeholders are informed about the project's progress, it is crucial to provide frequent and detailed updates. This includes sharing information about any achievements or milestones that have been reached, as well as any potential challenges that may arise in the future. When providing updates, it is important to be as thorough as possible, providing specific details about the work that has been completed, any roadblocks that have been encountered, and the steps that are being taken to address these challenges. This may include sharing metrics about the project's progress, such as timelines, budgets, or key performance indicators. By providing consistent and detailed updates, stakeholders will be able to stay informed about the project's progress and make informed decisions about how to proceed. This will also help to build trust and confidence among stakeholders, as they will see that you are committed to keeping them informed and engaged throughout the project lifecycle.

Adaptability in Communication: When communicating with clients, it is important to be mindful of their preferences and communication methods. By tailoring your communication style to suit each client, you can build stronger relationships, improve comprehension, and facilitate more productive interactions. Some clients may prefer more formal communication methods, such as email or written correspondence, while others may prefer more casual methods, such as phone calls or text messages. Additionally, some clients may prefer to communicate during specific times of the day or on specific days of the week. Understanding and accommodating these preferences can help you establish trust and rapport with your clients, ultimately leading to more successful and satisfying business relationships.

Empathy and Understanding: One of the key aspects of providing excellent customer service is always to strive to understand and empathize with your clients' perspectives. By doing so, you can foster a positive and collaborative relationship with them, which can help to build trust and loyalty over time. This means taking the time to actively listen to your client's concerns, asking questions to gain a deeper understanding of their needs, and being responsive to their feedback and suggestions. By showing empathy and understanding towards your clients, you can create a more supportive and productive working environment, ultimately leading to better outcomes for everyone involved.

Conflict Resolution and Assertiveness: Address conflicts diplomatically and assertively to maintain professionalism and project momentum. Keep an open mind, be firm but respectful, and seek fair and reasonable resolutions. By doing so, you can become an expert at finding solutions that promote respect and keep your project on track.

These strategies aim to improve client relationships by fostering clear, empathetic, and proactive communication.

SETTING CLEAR EXPECTATIONS

"Setting Clear Expectations" involves establishing transparent guidelines and boundaries to ensure mutual understanding between you and your clients regarding project details, deliverables, timelines, and responsibilities.

Key components include:

Detailed Scope of Work: When outlining the scope of a project, it's important to be as clear and specific as possible to ensure that all parties involved have a comprehensive understanding of the work that needs to be done. This involves breaking down the project into smaller tasks, outlining the objectives and goals, and defining the expected outcome. It's also crucial to identify the specific services that will be provided and to specify what is excluded from the scope of work. By providing a detailed and comprehensive scope, all stakeholders will be on the same page and the project can proceed smoothly and efficiently.

When starting a project, it's important to have a plan to keep everything on track. Here are two important things to consider to make sure your project goes smoothly:

1. Timelines: Set realistic deadlines for different parts of the project. Make sure everyone knows what they need to do when they need to do it, and when it needs to be finished.

2. Communication: Decide how you and your team will talk to each other. Choose the best way to communicate, like email or video calls. Make sure everyone knows how often they need to check in with each other to stay on the same page.

Roles and Responsibilities: It's important to have clear communication about who does what when working together on a project. This means outlining what you expect from the other person and what they can expect from you. By doing this, everyone involved will have a better understanding of their responsibilities and what needs to be done to complete the project.

Please take note of the following points:

Revision and Feedback Procedures: This section will explain how we will work together to make changes or improvements to the project. It will also give information about how many revisions we can make and what to do if we need more.

Payment Terms: This section will explain how payments will be made. It will include information about rates when payments are due, and how you can make payments. It will also explain if there are any upfront payments or fees you need to pay before we start working on the project.

HANDLING REVISIONS AND FEEDBACK PROFESSIONALLY

HERE ARE THREE MAIN DETAILED POINTS ON "HANDLING REVISIONS AND FEEDBACK PROFESSIONALLY"

Attentive and Respectful Listening: When dealing with feedback from clients, it's important to keep an open mind and really try to understand their point of view. Take the time to listen carefully to what they have to say, ask questions to make sure you fully understand their expectations and concerns, and do your best to see things from their perspective. This will help you to provide better service and build stronger relationships with your clients.

Constructive and Timely Responses: When responding to, feedback it's important to approach it in a professional and constructive manner. This means acknowledging the client's point of view and actively listening to their concerns. It's important to discuss potential solutions or adjustments that can be made to address their feedback and to offer clear timelines for implementing any necessary revisions. Promptness is key when it comes to addressing feedback. Responding to the client in a  timely manner demonstrates your commitment to their satisfaction and responsiveness to their needs. It's important to prioritize their feedback and ensure that it is addressed promptly and effectively. Being prompt in addressing feedback is crucial. It shows your commitment to the client's satisfaction and responsiveness to their needs. Prioritize their feedback and address it effectively to enhance your relationship with the client and improve your work. Keep an open mind and remain flexible when discussing potential solutions.

Quality-Focused Revisions and Transparent Communication: When revising work, it is important to prioritize the execution of revisions while upholding the quality of work. This means that you should focus on making the necessary changes as efficiently as possible while ensuring that the revised deliverables meet the highest standards of quality. To ensure that the revised deliverables align with the client's expectations and effectively address their concerns, it is essential to have a clear understanding of their needs and requirements. This can be achieved by reviewing the client's feedback and comments and incorporating their suggestions and ideas into the revised work.

Maintaining transparent communication throughout the revision process is also crucial. This involves providing regular updates to the client to showcase progress and ensure alignment with their needs. It is important to keep the client informed about any changes or developments and to address any questions or concerns they may have. Ultimately, the key to successful revisions is to strike a balance between efficiency and quality, while keeping the client's needs and expectations at the forefront. By following these guidelines and maintaining open communication with the client, you can ensure that the revised work meets their expectations and achieves the desired outcome.

OPTIMIZING FOR SUCCESS

"Optimizing for Success" is an approach to achieving your goals and reaching your full potential. It involves a variety of methods to help you perform at your best, seize opportunities, and obtain desired results. This approach requires evaluating your strategies, processes, and skills, making changes to improve them, and staying open to new ideas and ways of doing things.

To be successful, it's important to have clear goals in mind and take actions that align with them. This helps you focus your energy and make progress towards achieving specific milestones or targets. It's also important to have a positive attitude towards challenges, seeing them as opportunities for learning and growth.

To optimize for success, you need to use the resources available to you efficiently. This means staying up-to-date with the latest trends and best practices in your industry and using technology to your advantage. By continuously learning, adapting to change, and refining your strategies and processes, you can achieve personal or professional excellence over time.

by abdul rauf

LEVERAGING FIVERR ANALYTICS

"Leveraging Fiverr Analytics" involves utilizing the platform's analytical tools and data insights to understand performance, enhance strategy, and maximize success as a freelancer.

Key components of leveraging Fiverr Analytics include:

1. Performance Assessment: Use analytics to evaluate the performance of your gigs. Analyze metrics like views, clicks, and conversions to understand which gigs perform well and identify areas for improvement.

2. Client Behavior Analysis: Analyze client behavior patterns, including their preferences, search patterns, and purchasing trends. This helps you tailor your services to align with client needs.

3. Identifying Trends and Opportunities: Use analytics to identify market trends and emerging opportunities within your niche. This allows you to proactively adapt your services to meet changing demands.

4. Optimizing Gig Presentation: Based on analytics data, optimize your gig titles, descriptions, images, and pricing strategies. Make data-driven decisions to enhance your gig visibility and attract more clients.

5. Tracking Progress and Iterating Strategies: Monitor the effectiveness of changes made based on analytics insights. Continuously iterate and refine strategies to improve gig performance and overall success.

6. Understanding Client Preferences: Analyze data to understand what clients are searching for and tailor your gigs to match these preferences. This helps in crafting gigs that resonate with your target audience.

7. Strategic Decision-Making: Use analytics to inform strategic decisions about gig offerings, pricing, and promotional strategies. Employ data insights to make informed choices for business growth.

Using Fiverr Analytics can help freelancers improve their gig offerings, make informed decisions, and position themselves in the marketplace.

IMPLEMENTING SEO TECHNIQUES FOR GIGS

If you are a freelancer who offers services on Fiverr, it is important to make sure that your gigs are visible and easy to find for potential clients. One way to achieve this is by implementing SEO techniques for your gigs. SEO stands for Search Engine Optimization, which means making some changes to your gig's title, description, and tags to improve its ranking on Fiverr's search results page.

Here are some key steps to follow when implementing SEO techniques for your gigs:

Use relevant keywords: Think about the words your potential clients might use to search for the kind of services you offer, and make sure to include them in your gig's title, description, and tags.

Write a clear and catchy gig title: Your gig's title should accurately describe the services you offer, while also being attractive and easy to understand for potential clients.

Create a detailed gig description: Your gig's description should explain your services, expertise, and what makes you unique. Make sure to use relevant keywords, but also write it in a way that is easy to read and understand.

Use tags wisely: Fiverr allows you to add tags to your gig, which are keywords that describe your services. Make sure to select tags that are relevant to your services and align with popular search terms.

Use high-quality visuals: Your gig should include high-quality images or videos that showcase your work. Make sure to use descriptive filenames and alt texts that include relevant keywords.

Regularly update and optimize: Keep an eye on your gig's performance and make necessary adjustments to improve its ranking. You can update your gig's details, title, and keywords based on changing trends or to improve its search ranking.

Maintain high-quality standards: Your gig's content and services should consistently meet high-quality standards to ensure positive reviews and client satisfaction, which also contribute to improved search rankings.

Implementing effective SEO techniques can help freelancers to increase the visibility of their gigs on Fiverr. This can help them reach a broader audience and attract more potential clients interested in their services. The process of optimizing gigs on Fiverr involves continuous research, optimization, and staying updated with trends to maximize gig visibility and success on the platform.

UTILIZING FIVERR PROMOTIONS AND EXTRAS

Utilizing Fiverr's Promotions and Extras involves making use of the platform's tools for promoting your gigs and offering additional services to clients. Fiverr's promotional features help freelancers increase the visibility of their gigs by providing discounts, highlighted placements, or participation in platform-wide campaigns. By intelligently using these tools, you can attract more attention to your services, which can lead to more inquiries and orders. Furthermore, incorporating extras or add-on services within your gigs can make your services more valuable. These extras can include expedited delivery, expanded revisions, or supplementary services related to your primary offering.

Effectively presenting these extras can increase client satisfaction and encourage higher sales by catering to varying client needs and preferences. In short, leveraging Fiverr Promotions and Extras involves using the available tools strategically to increase your gig's visibility, attract more clients, and offer customized services that cater to diverse client requirements.

This can help you generate more sales opportunities and improve your success on the platform.

GROWING YOUR FREELANCE BUSINESS

If you're a freelancer on Fiverr, you need a reliable guide that can help you grow your business and advance your career. That's where "Growing Your Freelance Business" comes in handy. This chapter provides a strategic roadmap designed to assist freelancers in every stage of their journey, from beginners looking for their niche to experienced professionals aiming for higher levels of success.

This comprehensive guidebook will help you navigate through the complexities of building a thriving freelance business on Fiverr. It includes essential strategies, such as analyzing the market, building strong relationships with clients, diversifying your services, improving your efficiency, enhancing your marketing skills, and continuously improving your skills.

You'll find valuable insights that are tailored to Fiverr's unique landscape, blending market analysis with actionable steps to position yourself strategically, forge strong client relationships, expand your services, streamline your operations, and enhance your brand presence. With expert guidance, practical tips, and real-world examples, this guidebook is crafted to empower Fiverr freelancers. You'll learn how to grow your business, attract more clients, and foster sustained growth and success in the vibrant Fiverr freelance ecosystem.

SCALING YOUR SERVICES

When it comes to "Scaling Your Services" on Fiverr, there are several key strategies to keep in mind:

Diversification of Offerings: Consider expanding your service offerings by identifying related services within your area of expertise. This can help attract a broader client base and increase your earning potential.

Specialization in Niches: To stand out in a competitive marketplace, focus on specialized areas or niches where your expertise shines. This can help you establish yourself as a go-to provider in a particular field.

Upselling and Add-Ons: To provide additional value and cater to varying client needs, consider introducing add-on services or extras to your primary offering. This can help increase your revenue per client.

Creating Service Packages: Bundle related services together to offer comprehensive solutions, attracting clients seeking more extensive services. This can also help simplify your offerings and make it easier for clients to understand what you have to offer.

Listening to Feedback and Monitoring Trends: Pay attention to client feedback and market trends to identify areas for service expansion or improvement. This can help you stay ahead of the curve and ensure that you're meeting the evolving needs of your clients.

By implementing these strategies, Fiverr freelancers can expand their services, reach a wider audience and increase their competitiveness on the platform.

EXPANDING YOUR CLIENT BASE

If you are a freelancer on Fiverr, it's essential to attract new clients to grow your business. Here are some key strategies that can help you expand your client base:

1. **Targeted Marketing:** You can use marketing strategies to reach potential clients. For example, you can create content or advertise on social media to attract specific groups of people or businesses.
2. **Leverage Fiverr's Features:** Fiverr has many features that can help you attract potential clients. You can use buyer requests, promotional tools, and optimized gig listings to make your services visible to people browsing the platform.
3. **Networking and Referrals:** Networking with other freelancers or professionals in your industry can lead to referrals or recommendations for new clients. You can engage with peers, join forums, or attend relevant events to find new client opportunities.
4. **Offering Incentives:** You can offer introductory discounts, referral bonuses, or special deals to attract new clients and encourage them to engage with your services.
5. **Showcasing Testimonials and Reviews:** You can highlight positive reviews and testimonials from satisfied clients on your Fiverr profile. Positive feedback can build credibility and attract new clients seeking reliable services.
6. **Continuous Professional Development:** You should stay updated with industry trends, upgrade your skills, and offer innovative services to appeal to a broader clientele seeking cutting-edge solutions.

By using these strategies, you can attract new clients, expand your reach, and build a sustainable client base on Fiverr.

MANAGING MULTIPLE ORDERS EFFICIENTLY

"Managing Multiple Orders Efficiently" is working on several projects at once while keeping the quality high, meeting deadlines, and ensuring everything runs smoothly on Fiverr. Here are some tips for doing it well:

- Prioritize and organize your tasks by how urgent and complex they are. Use tools like calendars and task managers to keep track of things.

- Communicate clearly with clients about how their project is going when it will be done, and any issues that come up.

- Make your work as efficient as possible by developing a system for talking to clients, making revisions, and delivering work. Avoid trying too many things at once, as this can make it hard to do your best work.

- Be realistic about how much work you can handle. Don't take on too much at once, or you might not be able to do a good job.

- Consider getting help from other people if you need it. You can outsource or delegate some tasks to others to manage your workload.

By following these tips, you can work on multiple projects at once and ensure everything gets done well and on time.

OVERCOMING CHALLENGES AND PITFALLS

As a freelancer on Fiverr, you might face many challenges while working. These can include things like competing with other freelancers, managing client expectations, dealing with revisions, managing your time, and handling changing workloads. To overcome these challenges, you need to have a proactive approach. This might involve improving the way you communicate with your clients, becoming better at managing your time, setting realistic expectations, and continuously learning new skills to manage your workload more efficiently. In order to succeed, you need to be resilient and view challenges as opportunities for growth. You also need to be adaptable, adjusting to changes in the industry, client needs, and market trends. It's important to learn from your past mistakes, understand what caused them, and use that knowledge to improve your strategies and processes. You can also seek support from other freelancers on Fiverr and look for mentors who can guide you along the way.

By committing yourself to continuous improvement, being resilient, and staying open to change, you can overcome the challenges of freelancing on Fiverr and achieve success.

DEALING WITH DIFFICULT CLIENTS

If you are dealing with difficult clients, there are certain things you can do to manage the situation effectively. First and foremost, it's important to remain calm, respectful, and professional in all your interactions with them. You should also pay close attention to their concerns and feedback, and try to understand their perspective before responding.

You should set clear and reasonable boundaries, such as what you can deliver, how many revisions you will do, and what communication channels you will use. This way, you can manage their expectations from the outset and avoid misunderstandings.

In your communication with the client, it's important to be transparent and clear about what you can and can't do, how long it will take, and any limitations you may have. If the client has concerns or issues, you should propose viable solutions to address them. You should collaborate with the client to find common ground and resolve conflicts amicably.

To avoid misunderstandings, it is important to keep a record of all communications and agreements made with difficult clients. If the client is continuously unreasonable or abusive, it may be necessary to respectfully end the professional relationship.

Dealing with clients can be a tricky business, but with the right mix of professionalism, effective communication, and a knack for creative problem-solving, you can turn even the most challenging interactions into win-win situations. So buckle up, take a deep breath, and get ready to navigate the choppy waters of client management like a pro!

TIME MANAGEMENT AND WORK-LIFE BALANCE

Managing time and balancing work and personal life are important aspects of our daily routine. Time management involves using our time wisely to get things done and meet deadlines. It includes setting priorities, planning schedules, and avoiding time-wasting activities so we can be more productive. On the other hand, work-life balance means finding a way to balance the time we spend on work and other aspects of our lives, such as family, hobbies, and relaxation. This helps us prevent burnout, stay healthy, and be happy. It's all about creating a good balance between our professional and personal responsibilities.

Successfully managing time and achieving work-life balance requires a few crucial steps. These include:

- **Setting Priorities:** It's essential to identify and prioritize tasks that are important and urgent to manage time effectively and avoid getting overwhelmed.

- **Planning and Organization:** Creating schedules, to-do lists, or using tools to organize tasks can help allocate time efficiently and avoid procrastination.

- **Setting Boundaries:** It's important to establish clear boundaries between work and personal life to prevent work from encroaching on personal time and vice versa.

- **Effective Delegation:** Delegating tasks when possible and seeking support or outsourcing tasks can help manage workload effectively.

- **Regular Breaks and Self-Care:** Taking regular breaks, incorporating self-care activities, exercise, and relaxation can help recharge and maintain mental and physical health.

- **Communication and Flexibility:** Communicating effectively with clients or employers about availability and being flexible while adhering to a structured routine is essential.

ADAPTING TO CHANGES IN FIVERR'S POLICIES AND ALGORITHM

Adapting to Changes in Fiverr's Policies and Algorithm requires freelancers to take certain steps. Here are three main ways to adapt:

1. **Continuous Awareness and Learning:** Adapting to Fiverr's policies and algorithms requires ongoing awareness and learning. Freelancers should stay updated through Fiverr's official announcements, forums, and newsletters. This involves understanding policy modifications and algorithm updates and how they affect gig visibility, ranking, and overall performance. By staying informed, freelancers can anticipate changes and adjust their strategies proactively to align with the evolving platform dynamics.

2. **Strategic Adjustments and Optimization:** Adapting involves strategic adjustments in response to policy changes or algorithmic updates. This includes modifying gig descriptions, refining keywords, optimizing pricing structures, and reevaluating service offerings to conform to new guidelines and improve visibility. It's a meticulous process of tweaking and fine-tuning strategies to maintain competitiveness amidst the dynamic environment of Fiverr, ensuring that gigs remain relevant and attractive to potential clients despite platform changes.

3. **Community Engagement and Resource Utilization:** Effectively adapting involves engaging with the Fiverr community, seeking insights from experienced freelancers, and utilizing available resources provided by Fiverr itself. Engaging in discussions and forums, or seeking guidance from peers can offer valuable perspectives and strategies to navigate policy changes or algorithmic shifts. Leveraging Fiverr's resources, such as guidelines, support documentation, or official announcements, provides critical information and tools to adapt more effectively, ensuring that freelancers can pivot and thrive despite platform alterations.

Freelancers can stay informed, make adjustments, and engage within the Fiverr community to adapt to policy and algorithm changes, ensuring continued competitiveness on the platform.

MASTERING FIVERR EXPERTISE

"Mastering Fiverr Expertise" refers to the comprehensive understanding and proficiency gained by freelancers in navigating and excelling within the Fiverr platform's ecosystem.

Mastering Fiverr expertise is a comprehensive approach aimed at honing skills, understanding platform intricacies, and maximizing potential within the Fiverr marketplace. It involves having a deep understanding of the platform's dynamics, algorithms, policies, and client behaviors.

To achieve mastery, freelancers need to follow these steps:

1. **Comprehensive Platform Understanding:** Freelancers must have a thorough understanding of the platform's features, algorithms, and policies. This includes staying updated with changes, knowing how the platform ranks gigs, and understanding the factors that impact visibility and success.

2. Optimized Gig Creation: Freelancers should create gigs that resonate with their target audience. This includes crafting compelling gig descriptions, using relevant keywords, setting competitive pricing, and using eye-catching visuals to attract potential clients.

3. Exceptional Service Delivery: Freelancers must deliver exceptional service consistently. This includes maintaining high-quality work standards, offering excellent customer service, and adhering to deadlines to ensure client satisfaction and positive reviews.

4. Adaptability and Improvement: Freelancers should be adaptable to changes in the platform's algorithms, policies, and market trends. It also involves a commitment to continual improvement by learning new skills, refining existing ones, and staying updated with industry best practices.

5. Strategic Networking and Brand Building: Freelancers must engage in strategic networking within the community, foster relationships, and establish a strong brand presence. Engaging with the Fiverr community, participating in forums, and seeking mentorship opportunities contribute to mastering expertise.

6. Data-Driven Optimization: Freelancers should use data analytics to track performance metrics, understand client behaviors, and optimize gig performance. This involves analyzing impressions, clicks, conversions, and other metrics to make informed decisions for continuous improvement.

Achieving mastery in Fiverr expertise is an ongoing journey that requires dedication, adaptability, continuous learning, and a commitment to delivering exceptional services. By mastering these elements, freelancers can stand out, attract more clients, and establish a successful and sustainable career on Fiverr.

ADVANCED STRATEGIES FOR SUCCESS

Adapting to Changes in Fiverr's Policies and Algorithm requires freelancers to take certain steps. Here are three main ways to adapt:

1. **Continuous Awareness and Learning:** Adapting to Fiverr's policies and algorithms requires ongoing awareness and learning. Freelancers should stay updated through Fiverr's official announcements, forums, and newsletters. This involves understanding policy modifications and algorithm updates and how they affect gig visibility, ranking, and overall performance. By staying informed, freelancers can anticipate changes and adjust their strategies proactively to align with the evolving platform dynamics.

2. **Strategic Adjustments and Optimization:** Adapting involves strategic adjustments in response to policy changes or algorithmic updates. This includes modifying gig descriptions, refining keywords, optimizing pricing structures, and reevaluating service offerings to conform to new guidelines and improve visibility. It's a meticulous process of tweaking and fine-tuning strategies to maintain competitiveness amidst the dynamic environment of Fiverr, ensuring that gigs remain relevant and attractive to potential clients despite platform changes.

3. **Community Engagement and Resource Utilization:** Effectively adapting involves engaging with the Fiverr community, seeking insights from experienced freelancers, and utilizing available resources provided by Fiverr itself. Engaging in discussions and forums, or seeking guidance from peers can offer valuable perspectives and strategies to navigate policy changes or algorithmic shifts. Leveraging Fiverr's resources, such as guidelines, support documentation, or official announcements, provides critical information and tools to adapt more effectively, ensuring that freelancers can pivot and thrive despite platform alterations.

Freelancers can stay informed, make adjustments, and engage within the Fiverr community to adapt to policy and algorithm changes, ensuring continued competitiveness on the platform.

Reaching the status of a "Top-Rated Seller" or "Fiverr Pro" on the Fiverr platform is a significant achievement that represents the highest level of success. It comes with a range of exclusive opportunities and elevated status on the platform, giving sellers more visibility and credibility to attract potential buyers.

Here's an overview:

Earning the title of Top-Rated Seller or obtaining Fiverr Pro status is a testament to a freelancer's exceptional performance, reliability, and quality of service on the platform.

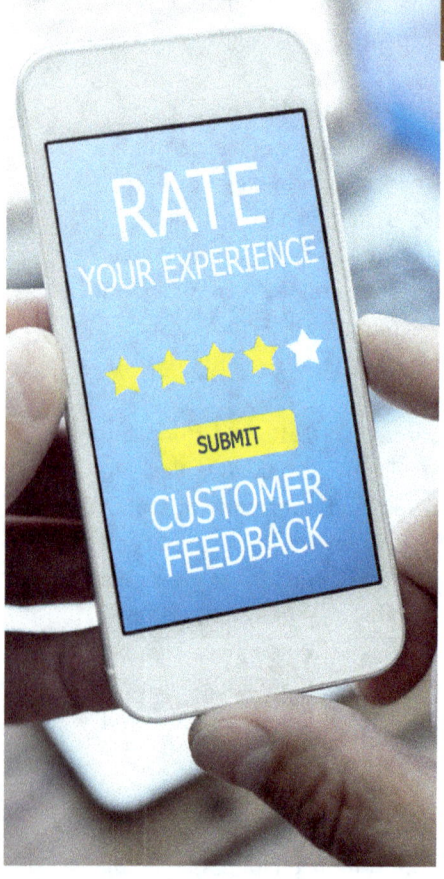

TOP-RATED SELLER STATUS:

- **Exceptional Performance:** Top-rated sellers consistently deliver high-quality work, receive exceptional reviews, maintain a high completion rate, and uphold Fiverr's standards.
- **Reliability and Trust:** Want to know what makes this team stand out from the rest? It's simple - clients trust them for their unwavering reliability, outstanding professionalism, and an unbreakable commitment to delivering quality work on time, every time. With a track record of exceeding expectations consistently, it's no wonder they are a go-to choice for many happy clients!
- **Privileges and Benefits:** Top-rated sellers receive exclusive benefits including increased visibility in search results, VIP support, promotional opportunities, and eligibility for the Fiverr Pro program.

Fiverr Pro Status:

Elite Professionalism: Fiverr Pro represents a group of highly professional and skilled freelancers who provide exceptional services in their respective fields.

Rigorous Selection Process: Fiverr Pro is a distinguished community of highly skilled freelancers who epitomize professionalism, expertise, and quality in their respective fields. Their exceptional work is a testament to their unwavering commitment to delivering top-tier services and exceeding client expectations. If you seek to partner with the finest freelancers, Fiverr Pro is the go-to platform for you.

Premium Services: Fiverr Pro sellers provide high-quality services with reliability, expertise, and professionalism. They are the go-to option for clients looking for top-notch quality and specialized skills.

Benefits of Top-Rated Seller or Fiverr Pro Status:

- **Increased Visibility and Trust:** Fiverr is a popular marketplace for freelancers to offer their services. To stand out and attract potential clients, achieving certain statuses on the platform is important. These statuses not only increase visibility but also instill trust among clients who are looking for high-quality services.
- **Access to Premium Opportunities:** Did you know that Top-Rated Sellers and Fiverr Pro freelancers enjoy exclusive gigs, work with premium clients, and land high-paying projects? It's true! With these perks, you can take your freelance career to the next level. Exciting, isn't it?
- **Distinguished Branding:** The status badge is a symbol of trust and assurance that customers can rely on when doing business with a seller. It distinguishes sellers from their peers and indicates a high level of professionalism and service quality.

Top-Rated Seller or Fiverr Pro status is a recognition of a freelancer's hard work, professionalism, and dedication. It brings various benefits, such as access to premium opportunities, higher visibility, and a better reputation within the Fiverr community.

CONTINUOUS LEARNING AND SKILL DEVELOPMENT

Continuous learning and skill development is an ongoing process that individuals, particularly freelancers, undertake to consistently seek new knowledge, refine existing expertise, and adapt to emerging trends within their industry. This pursuit involves adopting a lifelong growth mindset, actively pursuing new knowledge, refining existing skills, remaining adaptable and relevant, and applying acquired knowledge and skills into practical work scenarios.

A lifelong growth mindset involves embracing an attitude that values ongoing improvement and sees learning as a continuous journey rather than a finite destination. It involves acknowledging that skills require constant honing to stay competitive.

To actively pursue new knowledge, individuals can seek out new information, innovative methodologies, and evolving industry trends. This can be achieved through enrollment in courses, attending workshops, reading industry-related materials, or engaging in self-study to expand skill sets.

Refinement of existing skills involves dedication to consistently practicing, enhancing, and mastering current abilities to achieve higher levels of proficiency.

Remaining adaptable and relevant entails staying abreast of industry shifts, technological advancements, and changes in consumer preferences. Individuals should adapt their skill sets to remain pertinent and address the ever-evolving needs of the market.

Finally, application and practical integration involve implementing acquired knowledge and skills into practical work scenarios. This includes applying new insights to improve service quality, increase efficiency, and foster innovation in service delivery.

In essence, continuous learning and skill development are pivotal for freelancers to remain adaptable, innovative, and competitive in their field. It's a deliberate effort that ensures professionals stay relevant and excel in an ever-evolving landscape, delivering high-quality services and meeting the demands of an ever-changing marketplace.

LEGAL AND FINANCIAL CONSIDERATIONS

"Legal and Financial Considerations" refer to important factors that freelancers should take into account regarding the law, money matters, and safeguarding their business interests in the world of freelance work.

1. Legal Compliance:

- As a freelancer, it's important to be aware of the legal requirements to operate your business. This includes things like registering your business, paying taxes, and obtaining the necessary licenses to do your work.
- You should also understand your rights when it comes to things like your creative work and know what kind of contracts and liabilities come with the services you provide.

2. Contractual Agreements:

- Creating and understanding contracts to protect both freelancers and clients.
- Defining what work will be done, how much and when will be paid, and what to do in case of disagreements or issues. All to make sure everyone involved in a project understands what is expected and what they can expect in return.

3. Financial Management:

- A well-organized financial system is critical for any business to keep track of income, manage expenses efficiently, and create effective budget plans.
- Furthermore, businesses must plan for taxes, manage invoices, and allocate funds for taxes and business growth to ensure they stay on top of their financial obligations.

4. Insurance and Risk Management:

- Businesses need to assess potential risks and acquire appropriate insurance coverage, such as liability or professional indemnity insurance, to mitigate those risks. Additionally, creating contingency plans to handle unforeseen circumstances that may affect the business is crucial.

5. Intellectual Property Protection:
- Safeguarding intellectual property rights through copyrights, trademarks, or patents.
- Understanding and protecting the ownership of created work to prevent unauthorized use or reproduction.

6. Compliance with Freelance Platforms:
- Adhering to the terms and conditions set by freelance platforms like Fiverr or Upwork to ensure compliance and avoid potential account issues.

7. Financial Planning and Investment:
- Planning for long-term financial stability, retirement, and investment opportunities.
- Seeking professional advice for wealth management and diversifying income streams for financial security.

For freelancers, it is crucial to have a thorough understanding of the legal and financial considerations that come with running a business. This knowledge is essential for protecting their business, ensuring legal compliance, and managing their finances effectively. By addressing these considerations, freelancers can mitigate risks, establish credibility, and lay the foundation for a sustainable and successful freelance career.

UNDERSTANDING FIVERR'S TERMS OF SERVICE

If you are a freelancer using Fiverr, you must be aware of the rules and guidelines governing your interaction and conduct on the platform. These rules are called Fiverr's Terms of Service. They cover the following areas:

- How to behave while using Fiverr, and what activities are not allowed. For example, you can't cheat, spam, or steal someone else's work.

- What services can you offer on Fiverr, and what services are not allowed? This ensures that everything offered on Fiverr is legal and ethical.

- How payments work, including fees and refunds. This helps to make sure that everyone gets paid fairly and on time.

- What responsibilities do buyers and sellers have, how to communicate, and how to resolve disputes? This ensures that everyone has a good experience on Fiverr.

- How to protect your work and respect others' work. This is important for intellectual property rights and copyright issues.

- How to create and maintain your Fiverr account, and how to keep it secure. This helps to ensure that your personal information is protected.

Finally, Fiverr can change these rules from time to time, so it's important to stay up-to-date.

It's important for freelancers who use Fiverr to follow the rules of the platform so that they don't get in trouble or have any issues with their account. To do this, it's a good idea to read the rules carefully and check for updates every once in a while. This will help freelancers stay informed and maintain a good reputation in the Fiverr community.

TAXATION, INVOICING, AND RECORD-KEEPING

As a freelancer, it's essential to stay on top of your finances, and that means managing taxation, invoicing, and record-keeping. These three elements are critical to your financial well-being, legal compliance, and overall success as a freelancer. Proper management of these aspects can help you navigate financial challenges, avoid penalties, and establish a solid foundation for a thriving freelance career.

Taxation:

If you're a freelancer, you need to be aware of your income tax obligations and make sure you pay the right amount. This includes self-employment taxes, which can be a bit confusing. It's important to follow the tax laws in your area so you can accurately report and pay taxes on the money you earn.

Invoicing:

Creating well-crafted invoices that outline the services provided, and payment terms, and maintaining clear communication with clients can significantly enhance the payment process efficiency and uphold a professional image for your business.

Record-Keeping:

Keeping track of all your financial information, like how much money you make and spend, and the documents you need for taxes, is important. It helps you stay organized and ensures that you file your taxes correctly.

If you work for yourself as a freelancer, it's important to keep track of your taxes, invoices, and records. This helps you stay financially secure and follow the rules.

PROTECTING YOUR FREELANCE BUSINESS LEGALLY

"Protecting Your Freelance Business Legally" means taking important steps to secure your freelance work, follow the law, and protect your business interests. Some of the key things you can do include:

1. **Business Structure Selection:**
- When starting a business, it's essential to select the appropriate legal framework that aligns with your business aspirations and provides adequate liability protection. Various legal structures, such as sole proprietorship, LLC, and others, have their advantages and disadvantages. Thus, it's crucial to understand the differences between each structure and choose the one that best suits your business objectives and offers the necessary legal protection.

2. **Contracts and Agreements:**
- One of the most crucial aspects of any project is to ensure that all parties involved are on the same page. This requires crafting comprehensive contracts that clearly outline the project scope, timelines, and payment terms. By doing so, potential disputes can be preempted, saving everyone time, money, and frustration.
- Additionally, it's important to enforce confidentiality and non-disclosure agreements to protect any sensitive information that may be involved in the project. This helps to ensure that the project runs smoothly and that all parties are satisfied with the outcome.

3. **Intellectual Property Rights:**
- It is important to secure copyrights, trademarks, or patents for your original work to prevent unauthorized use. Clearly defining ownership and usage rights in client agreements is also crucial to protect your created work. By taking these steps, you can safeguard your intellectual property and avoid any potential legal disputes.

4. **Insurance Coverage:** It is important to assess the potential risks associated with your business or profession. Once identified, it is advisable to acquire suitable insurance coverage such as professional liability and general liability insurance. These types of insurance can offset financial liabilities that may arise due to unexpected circumstances. Insurance coverage can secure your financial well-being and ensure a secure future for your business or profession.

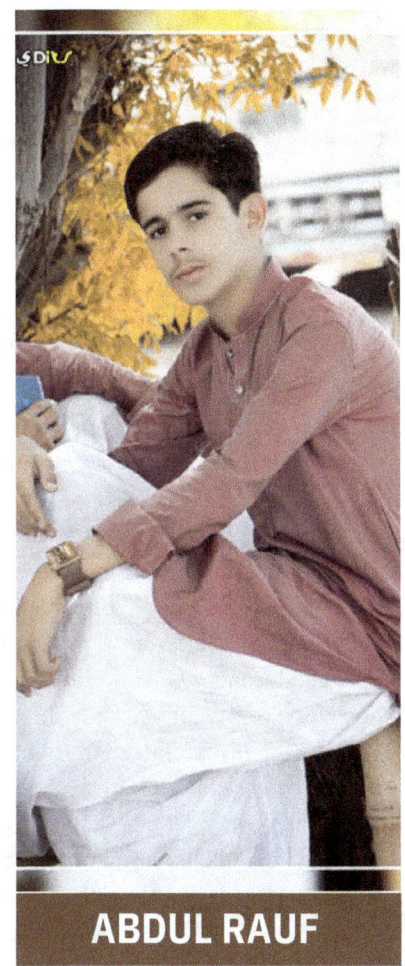

ABDUL RAUF

5. Compliance with Regulations:

- As a freelancer, it's crucial to stay up-to-date with the regulations and legal requirements specific to your industry. This includes adhering to labor laws, data protection regulations, and other mandates that may impact your work. By staying informed and compliant, you can ensure that you're operating legally and ethically in your freelance niche.

6. Dispute Resolution and Legal Counsel:

- Contracts should include mechanisms for resolving conflicts and seeking professional advice for legal issues.

7. Financial Prudence:

- Maintain transparent financial records, segregate personal and business finances, and adhere to tax laws to ensure accurate and timely filing of returns.

Legal precautions are crucial for shielding your freelance business from risks, establishing clear contractual terms, preserving intellectual property, and ensuring long-term success. Seeking legal guidance and implementing these measures proactively fortifies your business and maintains its industry reputation.

CONCLUSION

As we come to the end of our comprehensive journey through the world of freelancing, I want to reiterate the key takeaways that we have learned. Building a successful freelance career requires a holistic understanding of the essential pillars that underpin it. These pillars include legal security, intellectual property protection, financial prudence, client relations, continuous learning, and sustainable business growth. To establish a robust framework for your freelance business, it's crucial to prioritize legal safeguards that protect your interests and rights. You should also be vigilant about protecting your creative assets by registering your work and taking measures to prevent plagiarism and intellectual property theft. Managing your finances astutely is another essential aspect of freelancing. You should be proactive in tracking your income and expenses, setting realistic rates, and budgeting for your business's growth and sustainability. Fostering healthy client relationships is critical to your success as a freelancer. You should communicate transparently, deliver high-quality work on time, and establish clear boundaries to avoid misunderstandings and conflicts. Continuous learning is essential to keep up with industry trends, hone your skills, and stay competitive. You should invest in professional development opportunities, such as online courses and mentorship programs, to enhance your knowledge and expertise. Finally, achieving steady yet risk-conscious growth is critical to building a sustainable freelance business. You should focus on acquiring new clients, expanding your services, and diversifying your income streams while being mindful of the risks and challenges that come with growth.

By comprehending and integrating these fundamental principles, you'll have a solid foundation to navigate the intricate terrain of freelance entrepreneurship. Remember to implement these core elements into your freelance business to forge a resilient path toward a thriving and fulfilling career.

RECAP OF KEY LEARNINGS

The chapter titled **"Recap of Key Learnings"** is a vital section of any ebook that aims to summarize and synthesize the critical insights, lessons, and significant takeaways covered throughout the book. This chapter condenses and highlights the essential points discussed in each earlier chapter, providing readers with a quick reference or reminder of the most valuable information presented in the book.

Typically, this section includes a concise recapitulation of the main concepts, strategies, and actionable tips discussed in earlier chapters. It acts as a comprehensive review to reinforce the fundamental principles, strategies, and practices that are vital for succeeding as a freelancer on the Fiverr platform.

The "Recap of Key Learnings" chapter often outlines actionable steps or recommendations derived from the preceding chapters, empowering readers to apply the knowledge gained and implement effective strategies in their freelance endeavors on the Fiverr platform. This section is particularly useful for readers who may have skipped or missed some of the earlier chapters, as it provides a quick overview of the most important concepts and strategies they need to succeed in their freelance careers.

Overall, the **"Recap of Key Learnings"** chapter is an essential component of any ebook that aims to help readers learn and apply practical skills. It serves as a valuable tool for consolidating and summarizing the most critical information presented in the earlier parts of the book, enabling readers to apply what they have learned and achieve success in their chosen fields.

ENCOURAGEMENT AND NEXT STEPS

The section called "Encouragement and Next Steps" is a part of a book that helps readers stay motivated and plan their next steps after reading the book. This section usually includes tips and advice on how to move forward and take action on what they have learned from the book. It aims to encourage readers to keep going and achieve their goals.

11. Motivational Insights: This section typically includes uplifting phrases, motivational sayings, or stories that aim to increase the reader's self-assurance, reaffirm their abilities, and cultivate a positive outlook towards their work as a freelancer.

2. Actionable Guidance: The ebook is designed in a way that offers concrete and effective measures for readers to put into action as soon as they finish reading. These measures may take the form of practical guidelines, activities, or assignments that enable readers to transform theoretical knowledge into practical application.

3. Continued Learning and Growth: The text highlights the significance of constantly learning and developing oneself in the field of freelancing. It could recommend helpful sources, programs, groups, or websites where people can expand their abilities and understanding.

4. Setting Goals and Objectives: The ebook recommends setting achievable goals, both for the short-term and long-term, based on the insights gained from it. It may also guide how to set goals that work well for freelancing on Fiverr.

5. Support and Community Engagement: It's important to get support, connect with other people, and be a part of online communities where Fiverr freelancers hang out. This can help you learn from others, share your own experiences, and get advice to grow your freelancing career. The "Encouragement and Next Steps" section at the end of the article offers tips and guidance to help you stay motivated and take action to succeed in your Fiverr freelancing journey.

CONTACT US

ARE YOU INTERESTED IN EARNING MONEY ONLINE, BUT NOT SURE WHERE TO START? WE CAN PROVIDE YOU WITH PERSONALIZED GUIDANCE TO HELP JUMPSTART YOUR JOURNEY. OUR EXPERT, ABDUL RAUF, OFFERS ONE-ON-ONE ASSISTANCE TO PROVIDE YOU WITH INSIGHTS, STRATEGIES, AND TAILORED SUPPORT TO HELP YOU SUCCEED. DON'T HESITATE TO CONTACT US TODAY TO LEARN MORE ABOUT HOW WE CAN HELP YOU EARN MONEY ONLINE.

CONTACT US